MICROSOFT
EXCEL 5
FOR WINDOWS

PUBLISHED BY

Microsoft Press
A Division of Microsoft Corporation
One Microsoft Way
Redmond, Washington 98052-6399

Library of Congress Cataloging-in-Publication Data
Nelson, Stephen L., 1959-
  Field guide to Microsoft Excel for Windows /Stephen L. Nelson.
      p.   cm.
  Includes index.
  ISBN 1-55615-579-4
  1. Microsoft Excel for Windows. 2. Business -- Computer Programs.
3. Electronic spreadsheets. I. Title.
HF5548.4 M523N4523 1994
650'.0285'5369--dc20   93-44255
                                             CIP

Printed and bound in the United States of America

    3 4 5 6 7 8 9 QEQE 9 8 7 6 5

Distributed to the book trade in Canada by Macmillan of Canada, a division of Canada Publishing Corporation.

A CIP catalogue record for this book is available from the British Library.

Microsoft Press books are available through booksellers and distributors worldwide. For further information about international editions, contact your local Microsoft Corporation office. Or contact Microsoft Press International directly at fax (206) 936-7329.

Macintosh is a registered trademark of Apple Computer, Inc. Quattro is a registered trademark of Borland International, Inc. 1-2-3, Lotus, and Lotus Improv are registered trademarks of Lotus Development Corporation. WordPerfect is a registered trademark of WordPerfect Corporation.

Acquisitions Editor: Dean Holmes
Project Editor: Tara Powers-Hausmann
Technical Contact: Mary DeJong

FIELD GUIDE TO

MICROSOFT
EXCEL 5
FOR WINDOWS

Stephen L. Nelson

The Field Guide to Microsoft Excel version 5 is divided into four sections. These sections are designed to help you find the information you need quickly.

ENVIRONMENT

Terms and ideas you'll want to know to get the most out of Excel. All the basic parts of Excel 5 are shown and explained. The emphasis here is on quick answers, but most topics are cross-referenced so you can find out more if you want to.

Diagrams of key windows components, with quick definitions, cross referenced to more complete information.

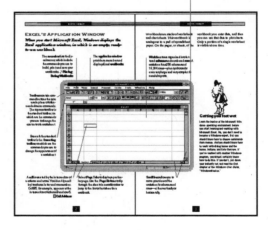

Tipmeister

Watch for me as you use this Field Guide. I'll point out helpful hints and let you know what to watch for.

13 EXCEL A TO Z

An alphabetic list of commands, tasks, terms, and procedures.

Step-by-step guides to performing most Excel tasks.

Quick identification of icons and groups.

Definitions of key concepts and terms, and examples of why you should know them.

Cross references to related topics.

139 TROUBLESHOOTING

A guide to common problems—how to avoid them, and what to do when they occur.

157 QUICK REFERENCE

Useful indexes, including a full list of menu commands, short-cut keys, and more.

179 INDEX

A complete reference to all elements of the Field Guide.

INTRODUCTION
● ●

*Sometime during grade school, my parents gave me
a field guide to North American birds. With its
visual approach, its maps, and its numerous
illustrations, that guide delivered hours of
enjoyment. The book also helped me better
understand and more fully appreciate
the birds in my neighborhood.
And the small book fit neatly in a child's rucksack.
But I'm getting off the track.*

HOW TO USE THIS BOOK

This book works in the same way as that field guide. It organizes information visually with numerous illustrations. And it does this in a way that helps you more easily understand and enjoy working with Microsoft Excel.

For new users, the field guide provides a visual path to the information necessary to start using Excel. But the field guide isn't only for beginners. For experienced users, the field guide provides concise, easy-to-find descriptions of Excel tasks, terms, and techniques.

WHEN YOU HAVE A QUESTION

Let me explain how to find the information you need. You'll usually want to flip first to the first section, Environment, which is really a visual index. You find the picture that shows what you want to do or the task you have a question about. If you want to build a worksheet, for example, you flip to pages 4 and 5, which show a worksheet.

Next, you read the captions that describe the parts of the picture—or the key elements of Excel. Say, for example, that you want to build a sales budget. The worksheet on pages 4 and 5 includes captions that describe how to enter textual descriptions and budgeted values. These key elements appear in **boldface** type to make them stand out.

WHEN YOU NEED MORE INFORMATION

You'll notice that some captions are followed by a little paw print and **boldface** terms. These refer to entries in the second section, Excel A to Z, and provide more information related to the caption's contents. (The paw print shows you how to track down the information you need. Get it?)

Excel A to Z is a dictionary of more than 200 entries that define terms and describe tasks. (After you've worked with Excel a bit or if you're already an experienced user, you'll often be able to turn directly to this section.) So, if you have just read the caption that says you can enter **formulas** into a worksheet, you can flip to the Formulas entry in Excel A to Z.

Any time an entry in Excel A to Z appears as a term within an entry, I'll **boldface** it the first time it appears in the entry. For example, as part of describing how formulas work, I might tell you that formulas can use a **cell address**. In this case, the words **cell address** will appear in bold letters—alerting you to the presence of a Cell Address entry. If you don't understand the term or want to do a bit of brushing up, you can flip to the entry for more information.

WHEN YOU HAVE A PROBLEM

The third section, Troubleshooting, describes problems that new or casual users of Excel often encounter. Following each problem description, I list one or more solutions you can employ to fix the problem.

WHEN YOU WONDER ABOUT A COMMAND

The fourth section, Quick Reference, describes each of the menu commands and the tools (buttons) on the Standard, Formatting, and Chart **toolbars**. If you want to know what a specific command or command button does, turn to the Quick Reference. (And don't forget about the index. You can look there to find all references in this book to any single topic.)

CONVENTIONS USED HERE

One final thing I should tell you is this: Rather than use wordy phrases such as, "Activate the File menu and then choose the Print command," I'm just going to say, "Choose the File Print command." Rather than say, "Select the Format Painter toolbar button from the Standard toolbar," I'm going to say, "Select the Format Painter Tool." (I'll show a picture of the toolbar button in the margin, too.) I also assume you know how to select menu commands, windows, and dialog box elements using either the mouse or the keyboard. No muss. No fuss.

ENVIRONMENT

Need to get the lay of the land quickly? Then the Environment is the place to start. It defines the key terms you'll need to know and the core ideas you should understand as you begin exploring Microsoft Excel.

EXCEL'S APPLICATION WINDOW

When you start Microsoft Excel, Windows displays the Excel application window, in which is an empty, ready-to-use workbook.

The menu bar lists the Excel menus, which include the commands you use to build, print, and save your workbooks.
❖ Printing; Saving Workbooks

The application window provides a menu bar and displays Excel **workbooks**.

Toolbars contain command buttons that you use in place of often-needed menu commands. The topmost toolbar is the Standard toolbar, on which are the commands you use to change the contents of a worksheet.

Beneath the Standard toolbar is the Formatting toolbar, on which are the commands you use to change the appearance of a worksheet.

A cell is created by the intersection of a column and a row. You identify a cell by its column letter and row number. Cell B5, for example, appears at the intersection of column B and row 5.
❖ Cell Address

Select Page Tabs to display a particular page. Use the Page Buttons to flip through the sheets in a workbook or to jump to the first or last sheet in a workbook.

Workbooks are stacks of worksheets and chart sheets. This workbook is analogous to a pad of spreadsheet paper. On the pages, or sheets, of the workbook, you enter data, and then you can use that data to plot charts. Only a portion of a single worksheet is visible at one time.

Worksheets are organized into lettered **columns** and numbered **rows**. A worksheet has 256 columns and 16,384 rows—plenty of room for even very large and very complex financial reports.

Getting your feet wet

Learn the basics of the Microsoft Windows operating environment before you start learning and working with Microsoft Excel. No, you don't need to become a Windows expert. But you should know how to choose commands from menus. And you should know how to work with dialog boxes and the boxes, buttons, and lists they use. If you've worked with another Windows program, you almost certainly know how to do this. If you don't, put down your butterfly net and read the first chapter of the Windows *User's Guide*, "Windows Basics."

Scroll bars allow you to move your view of the worksheet's columns and rows—either vertically or horizontally.

MICROSOFT EXCEL WORKSHEETS

Worksheets are the basic building blocks of workbooks. By entering information in the form of labels, values, and formulas into worksheet cells, you create tables, or spreadsheets, useful for summarizing, tabulating, and analyzing.

Labels are pieces of text. Often, you use labels to describe values stored in other cells.

Values are numbers you want to use in formulas. You also use values to represent dates.
❖ Date Values

Formulas can add, subtract, multiply, and divide values. Usually, these values are stored in another cell. To get a value stored in a cell, the formula uses the cell's address. This formula adds the values in cells B9, B10, B11, B13, B14, and B15.

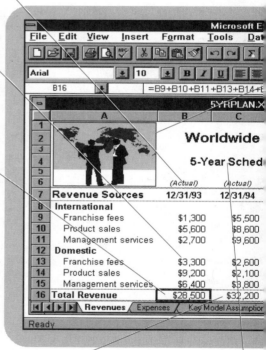

Numeric punctuation—dollar signs, commas, and decimals places—makes worksheet values easier to read.
❖ Formatting

Type style and size can be used to make characters and numbers in labels and values easier to read.You can also add border lines.
❖ Borders; Fonts; Points

To build a worksheet, you simply enter **labels**, **values**, and **formulas** into the cells of a worksheet. To do this, click on the cell, type what you want, and then press Enter. The unique feature of a spreadsheet program—such as Microsoft Excel—is its ability to calculate formulas.

When you enter a formula into a worksheet cell, Excel calculates the formula's result. If the formula uses values from other cells—the usual case—Excel recalculates the formula's result any time one of these values changes.

❖ **Calculating Formulas**

You can add pictures to worksheets—such as a company logo—if the picture is stored on disk as a graphic image. To do this, choose Insert Picture.

❖ **Worksheet Pictures**

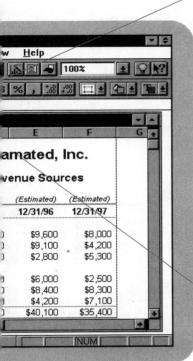

w	Help					
			100%			

amated, Inc.

venue Sources

	(Estimated)	*(Estimated)*
	12/31/96	**12/31/97**
	$9,600	$8,000
	$9,100	$4,200
	$2,800	$5,300
	$6,000	$2,500
	$8,400	$8,300
	$4,200	$7,100
	$40,100	$35,400

NUM

Quick and easy formatting

One easy way to add **formatting** is with the Format AutoFormat command. Simply select the worksheet area, or range, choose Format AutoFormat, and select a format.

Row heights and column widths can be adjusted to make space for long labels and large values.

❖ **Columns; Rows**

Excel provides default sheet names. To change these names, simply double-click the **Page Tab**; when Excel displays a dialog box, enter a name in the space provided.

MICROSOFT EXCEL CHARTS

Using Excel's ChartWizard, you can quickly create charts that visually depict worksheet data. Charts appear either as objects embedded in a worksheet or on their own workbook sheet.

A data category is the method you use to organize data series values. Usually, these are simply the time periods you use to plot the data series. Here, for example, the data category is months.

The sets of related values you will plot are called data series. This worksheet shows four "interest rate" data series: 3-month T-bill, 3-month CD, Commercial Paper, and 3-month Eurodollar.

Different chart types use different data markers: bars, pie slices, lines, and so on. You can easily change the chart type using the Chart toolbar or the Format Chart Type command. Excel differentiates the data markers for each data series. For example, on this chart, columns appear in different colors.

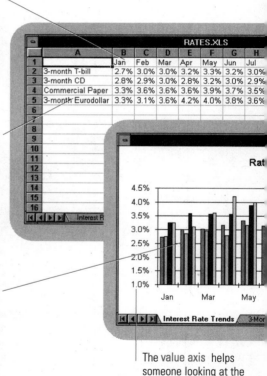

The value axis helps someone looking at the chart calibrate the plotted values. You can add value axis **gridlines** too.

To create a chart, you first build a worksheet that holds the to-be-plotted data. Then you select the data range (by dragging the mouse from the upper left corner to the lower right corner) and start the ChartWizard. So, what does the Chart Wizard do? It steps you through five dialog boxes that ask how Excel should plot your data.

You can add a chart title to summarize a chart's message or point out subtleties in the data. You can also add other text to label axes or annotate the chart.

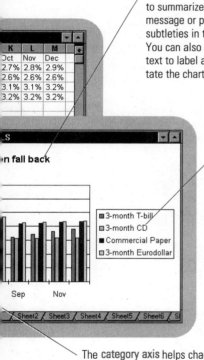

K	L	M
Oct	Nov	Dec
2.7%	2.8%	2.9%
2.6%	2.6%	2.6%
3.1%	3.1%	3.2%
3.2%	3.2%	3.2%

n fall back

■ 3-month T-bill
□ 3-month CD
■ Commercial Paper
□ 3-month Eurodollar

Sep   Nov

Sheet2 / Sheet3 / Sheet4 / Sheet5 / Sheet6 / Sl

Chart legends name the data series. Excel will use the data series names from your worksheet as long as you include these names in your worksheet selection. You can add and remove chart legends using the Chart toolbar.

The category axis helps chart viewers keep the data organized. Excel will use category names from your worksheet as long as you include these names in your worksheet selection. (Excel often uses every other category name to conserve space—as shown here.)

LIST MANAGEMENT

List Management is a simple yet handy database feature. A list is an organized set of similar chunks of information.

The first row names the fields of the list. Excel calls these headers. Each column stores the same information: Last names in column A, first names in column B, and so on.

To create a list, you use the rows and columns of a worksheet. In this example, each employee name goes into a separate row: Peter Abbot on the first row, Shalandra Borchert on the second row, and so on.
❖ **Creating Lists**

	A	B	C	D	E	F
					SALARIES.XLS	
1	Last Name	First Name	MI	Department	Salary	
2	Abbot	Peter	W	Sales	$14,000	
3	Borchert	Shalandra	P	Mfg	$18,000	
4	Chang	Geng	Y	Mfg	$36,000	
5	DeLaurenti	Anthony	L	Mfg	$34,000	
6	Edwards	Jennifer	B	Sales	$32,000	
7	Foles	Thomas	L	Sales	$8,000	
8	Gonzalez	Rachel	M	Sales	$40,000	
9	Hapsburg	Jackson	A	Acctg	$6,000	
10	Ito	Fumio	S	Acctg	$32,000	
11	Johnson	Geoffrey	C	Acctg	$20,000	
12	Kirkland	Ralph	E	Acctg	$47,000	
13	Land	Walter	O	Admin	$22,000	
14	Mercedes	Marie	C	Admin	$47,000	
15	Nagai	Patrick	T	Mfg	$16,000	
16	Olsenius	Aristotle	D	Mfg	$47,000	

Employee Salaries / Department Payroll Summary

This list shows only 15 entries, or records, and uses only 5 columns even though an Excel worksheet provides 16,384 rows and 256 columns. So you can store very large lists in a worksheet if your computer has enough memory and disk space.

You can arrange, or sort, list entries. For example, you can alphabetize a list by employee last names (as shown here). You can also organize a list in order of ascending or descending value fields (such as by salary).
❖ **Sorting Lists**

To build a list, you use a worksheet. Typically, you use a row for each list entry. Information stored in a list can be textual (for example, employee names) or numeric (for example, the salary amounts). You can also include formulas.

You can enter data directly into the worksheet by clicking a cell, typing, and pressing Enter, or you can use the Data Form command.

In the Data Form dialog box, you can enter and edit records into a list. To use it, select a list's headers and its entries and then choose the Data Form command. Excel uses the worksheet name to title the dialog box, and it uses the headers to label the text boxes provided in the dialog box.

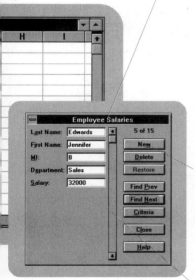

Select New to start a new entry with the Data Form dialog box, and then fill in the blank text boxes and move to the next record.

To edit the list entry displayed, edit the text box contents and move to the next record. You can page through the list using the PageUp and PageDown keys, the Find Next or Find Prev buttons, and the scroll bar.

9

PRINTING WORKBOOKS

You can print the worksheets and chart sheets as they appear on the screen. The same font styles and point sizes, border lines, and graphic images that appear on your screen will appear on the printed page.

You choose a page orientation that fits your worksheet or chart using the File Page Setup command's Page Tab. Often, worksheets and charts fit better if the page orientation is landscape, or horizontal, as shown here.

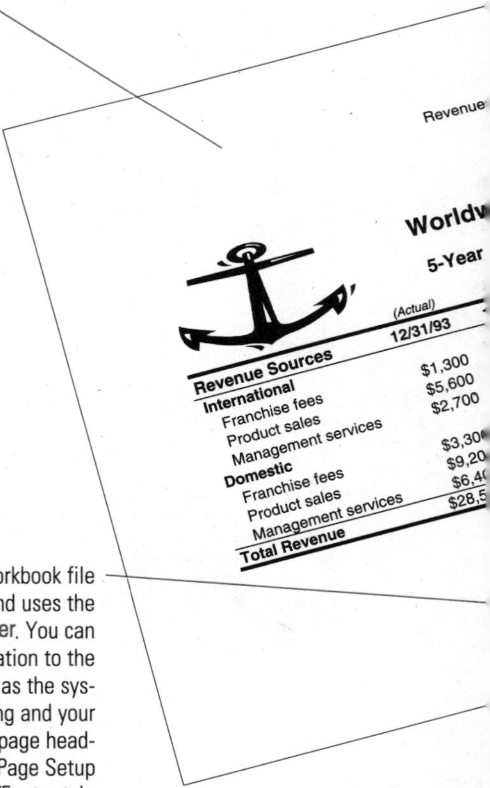

Revenue

Worldw

5-Year

(Actual)

12/31/93

Revenue Sources	
International	
Franchise fees	$1,300
Product sales	$5,600
Management services	$2,700
Domestic	$3,30
Franchise fees	$9,20
Product sales	$6,40
Management services	$28,5
Total Revenue	

By default, Excel uses the workbook file name as a page header and uses the page number as a page footer. You can add other bits of information to the header and footer too, such as the system date and time at printing and your company name. To change page headers and footers, use the File Page Setup command's Header/Footer tab.

❖ **Headers and Footers**

To print a worksheet or a chart, simply display it and then choose the File Print command. Excel displays a dialog box that asks what and how you want to print, but you can accept the default, or suggested, print settings by pressing Enter.
❖ **Printing**

amated, Inc.
evenue Sources

ed)	(Estimated)	(Estimated)
95	12/31/96	12/31/97
9,100	$9,600	$8,000
6,400	$9,100	$4,200
8,700	$2,800	$5,300
		$2,500
	$6,000	$8,300
$6,700	$8,400	$7,100
$5,000	$4,200	$35,400
$1,600	$40,100	
$37,500		

Previewing printed pages

You can see what your printed pages will look like without actually printing them. Just choose the File Print Preview command. Excel displays a window that shows a printed page and provides command buttons you can use to page through the document, adjust page settings (such as margins and footers), and initiate printing once things look right.
❖ Print Preview

Setting page margins controls where Excel prints on a page and how much room is available for printing. You can also tell Excel to print small worksheets and charts in the center of a page's print area. To control page margin settings, use the File Page Setup command's Margin tab.
❖ Page Setup

EXCEL A TO Z

Maybe it's not a jungle out there. But you'll still want keep a survival kit close at hand. Excel A to Z, which starts on the next page, is just such a survival kit. It lists in alphabetic order the tools, terms, and techniques you'll need to know.

Absolute Cell Address

An absolute cell address is simply a cell address you use in a formula but don't want adjusted when the formula is copied.

Creating Absolute Cell Addresses

Make the column and row components of a cell address absolute by preceding them with a dollar sign. For example, to make the cell address A1 absolute, insert dollar signs—A1.

Creating Mixed Cell Addresses

In a mixed cell address, only some components are absolute. To create a mixed cell address, simply precede those address components you want absolute with a dollar sign. For example, the cell address $A1 has only its column fixed, and the cell address A$1 has only its row fixed.

❖❖ **Formulas; Relative Cell Address**

The absolute key

When editing or entering a cell address, you can press F4 to change a cell address from relative to absolute, from absolute to mixed, and from mixed back to relative.

Active Cell

The active cell is the cell with the **cell selector,** or pointer (that dark border thingamajig that jumps from cell to cell as you press direction keys). If you type something and press Enter, Excel sticks what you type into the active cell. And the address of the active cell —the **cell reference**— is in the upper left corner below the Formatting toolbar.

You can always tell which cell is active by looking at the cell reference.

Excel also identifies the active cell with the cell selector, which is kind of handy.

Active and Inactive Windows

The active **application window**—such as the Excel application window—is the one that appears in front of all other open windows. (Cleverly, this is called the foreground. The inactive application windows, if there are inactive applications, appear in the background.)

The active workbook window is the one any Excel commands you choose will affect. You can tell which workbook window is active because its title bar will show in a different color (usually blue).

Activating Document Windows

To activate a different workbook window, click the window or choose the Window menu command that names the window.

Activating Application Windows

To activate a different application window, click the window or choose the Control menu's Switch To command.

Active Sheet

The active sheet is the one you can see in the workbook window and the sheet upon which selected commands act. Note too, my friend, that which sheet is active determines which menu bar Excel provides. For example, if a worksheet is active, Excel displays the worksheet menu bar; if a chart sheet is active, Excel displays the Chart menu bar.

Adding Styles

To add a style—a combination of formatting choices—to the open workbook, format a cell so that it uses the style and then choose the Format Style command.

1 In the Style Name combo box, name the style.

2 The Style Includes box shows the formatting choices that make up the Style Name. To remove formatting choices, unmark check boxes.

continues

Adding Styles *(continued)*

3 Select Add when the Style dialog box describes the formatting choices you want to combine as a style.

4 If you want to change a style, select it from the Style Name combo box, select Modify, and use the Format Cells dialog box that Excel displays.

Formatting

Deleting styles

If you inadvertently add a style you don't want, select it from the Style Name combo box and then click Delete.

Aligning Labels and Values
Alignment refers to how Excel positions **labels** and **values** in cells. Unless you tell it otherwise, Excel applies two simple alignment rules: left-align labels, and right-align values. You can override these rules with the Format Cells command. Follow these steps:

1 Select the cell or cells.

2 Choose the Format Cells command. Excel displays the Format Cells dialog box.

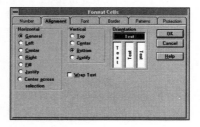

3 Select the Alignment tab. Excel displays the Format Cells Alignment tab options.

4 Use the Horizontal radio buttons to indicate how labels and values should be aligned to left and right edges of cell:

Choice	Result
General	The usual two rules are applied.
Left	Labels and values are left-aligned.
Center	Labels and values are centered between cells' left and right edges.
Right	Labels and values are right-aligned.
Fill	Labels are repeated in a cell as many times as they will fit.
Justify	Row height is adjusted and label is split into horizontal lines of text.
Center Across Selection	Labels and values are centered across the selected cells.

5 Turn on the Wrap Text check box if you want row heights adjusted and labels split into lines of text.

6 Use the Vertical radio buttons to indicate how labels and values should be aligned to top and bottom edges of cell:

Choice	Result
Top	Labels and values are aligned flush to top edge.
Center	Labels and values are centered between top and bottom edges.
Bottom	Labels and values are aligned flush to bottom edge.
Justify	Row height is adjusted and label is split into vertical lines of text.

7 Use the Orientation boxes to indicate how labels and values should appear in cells. (The boxes depict the alternatives.)

8 Select OK.

ANSI Characters

The ANSI character set includes all the **ASCII characters** your keyboard shows plus the special characters your keyboard doesn't show, such as the Japanese yen symbol, ¥, or the British pound symbol, £. Even though these special characters don't appear on your keyboard, you can still use them in Excel worksheets.

Adding ANSI Characters

To add ANSI characters, hold down Alt and, using the numeric keypad, enter the ANSI character code for the symbol. For example, the ANSI character code for the Japanese yen symbol is 0165. To enter a yen symbol into a worksheet, hold down Alt and type 0165 using the numeric keypad. (You can get ANSI character codes from the Windows user documentation.)

Application Window

The application window is the rectangle in which an application such as Excel displays its menu bar, toolbars, and any open workbook **document windows.**

Applying Styles

To apply, or use, a style, follow these steps:

1 Select the cells you want to format.

2 Choose the Format Style command. Excel displays the Style dialog box.

3 Select the style from the Style Name combo box.

4 If you don't want to use one of the formatting choices—Number, Font, Alignment, Border, Patterns, or Protection—unmark its check box.

5 Select OK.

 Formatting

Painting styles

You can copy a style from one worksheet range to another using the Format Painter toolbar button.

Argument An argument is a unit of information, or an input, used in a function. Arguments can be **labels, values, cell addresses,** cell names, **formulas,** and even other **functions.** Arguments are enclosed in parentheses and separated by commas. For example, the function that calculates a monthly loan payment uses a minimum of three inputs— the interest rate, the number of monthly payments, and the loan amount. If the annual interest rate is 8%, the loan is $5000, and number of years of monthly payments is 3, you could enter the following function:

=PMT(.08/12,3*12,5000)

The annual interest rate is 8%, or 0.08; so the monthly interest rate argument is 0.08/12—the annual interest rate divided by 12. The loan requires monthly payments over 3 years; so the payments argument is 3*12, which returns the number of monthly payments made over 3 years. The last argument, 5000, is the loan amount.

A handful of functions don't use inputs and, therefore, don't require arguments, for example, the function for calculating the mathematical constant pi. When a function doesn't use arguments, follow the function name with empty parentheses, as shown below with the pi function:

=PI()

.·. **Function Wizard**

Array An array is simply a set of numbers—such as those stored in a row or a column. You can use arrays in **array formulas** to return arrays. For example, you can add the array 1, 2, 3 to the array 4, 5, 6, and you get a new array 5, 7, 9.

Array 1:	1	2	3
+ Array 2:	4	5	6
= Array 3:	5	7	9

This makes sense, right? The first number, 5, is calculated by adding the first numbers in the two input arrays, 1 and 4.

continues

19

Array *(continued)*

The second number, 7, is calculated by adding the second numbers in the two input arrays, 2 and 5. And the third number, 9, is calculated by adding the third numbers in the two input arrays, 3 and 6.

Array Formulas

With handy and powerful array formulas you can write a single formula that makes several calculations. Sure, this sounds complicated, but a quick example will show you the basics of arrays and array formulas. Take a peek at the following worksheet chunk. Suppose, for the sake of illustration, that you want to multiply the values in each row of column A by the values in each row of column B. Multiplying the account balance in column A by the interest rate in column B, for example, would calculate the interest.

Writing an Array Formula

To create an array formula that makes this calculation, take these steps:

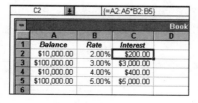

1 Select C2:C5.

2 Type the equals sign, =.

3 Select A2:A5.

4 Type the multiplication sign, *.

5 Select B2:B5.

6 Press Shift+Ctrl+Enter.

Excel enters the formula {=A2:A5*B2:B5} into each of the cells in C2:C5. This array formula tells Excel, "Calculate C2 by multiplying A2 by B2, calculate C3 by multiplying A3 by B3, calculate C4 by multiplying A4 by C4, and calculate C5 by multiplying A5 by B5." By the way, the arrays in an array formula must have the same number of values.

Editing an Array Formula

You edit an array formula in the same way you edit other formulas. For example, double-click one of the cells with the array formula; then make your changes. If you edit an array formula, Excel removes the braces as you edit; so you press Shift+Ctrl+Enter when you're done to tell Excel the formula is an array. By the way, if you edit one of the array formulas, Excel updates each of the formulas in the array.

 Array

About those braces

Note that you don't type the braces yourself to create an array formula; you press Shift+Ctrl+Enter, and Excel adds the braces for you.

ASCII Characters
The ASCII character set basically consists of the characters you see on your keyboard plus roughly a couple dozen other characters that you don't see, are unprintable, and you don't need to worry about anyway.

Excel provides text functions that manipulate ASCII characters, show which characters various ASCII codes represent, and show which ASCII codes return which characters.

As a general rule, you shouldn't have to worry all that much about ASCII characters if you're working with Excel. Why? You can type all the ASCII characters that you'll need with the keyboard.

ANSI Characters

ASCII Text Files
An ASCII text file is a text file that uses only **ASCII characters**. You can import one of these babies using the File Open command.

Delimited Text Files; Importing Text Files

Auditing Worksheets

In a worksheet, which values get used where can be perplexing. To ease the burden, Excel provides a set of error-checking tools, which you make available by choosing the Tools Auditing command: Trace Precedents, Trace Dependents, and Trace Error. These commands let you visually inspect relationships between **formulas** and the **values** used in formulas.

Tracing Precedents

The Auditing Trace Precedents command draws a blue arrow from the cells addressed by the active cell's formula to the active cell.

2	An input value	↑	1
3	Formula that uses input	↓	1

Tracing Dependents

You can see which cells depend on the active cell by using the Auditing Trace Dependents command. It draws a blue arrow from the active cell to cells addressing the active cell.

Tracing Errors

The Auditing Trace Error command draws arrows from cells addressed by an active cell's erroneous formula to the active cell. Excel draws red arrows from dependent cells holding error values, and blue arrows from all the other dependent cells.

6	An erroneous input	↑	#DIV/0!
7	Formula that uses input	↓	#DIV/0!

Two More Tools

Note that the Auditing submenu also provides two additional tools: Remove All Arrows, which erases the arrows you've added using the Trace commands, and Show Auditing Toolbar, which adds a toolbar for more quickly choosing auditing commands.

Dependents; Error Messages; Precedents

AutoFormatting Tables You can format a worksheet selection, or range, to follow a conventional set of formatting rules. To do so, follow these steps:

1 Build the table and then select it.

2 Choose the Format AutoFormat command.

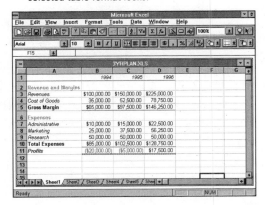

3 From the AutoFormat list box, select a Table Format. Here I've selected the Accounting 3 format. The Sample box shows how the selected table format looks.

4 Select OK. The figure shows an example worksheet range after using the Format AutoFormat command. Nice, huh? (This is the same worksheet range shown above step 1—only autoformatted using the Accounting 3 format.)

AutoSave You can tell Excel it should automatically save your workbooks on a regular basis with the AutoSave add-in.

Turning on AutoSave

To do this, choose the Tools AutoSave command and follow these steps:

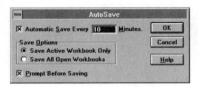

1 Mark the Automatic Save check box to turn on Excel's automatic file-saving feature.

2 Specify how often the workbook file should be saved using the Every Minutes combo box.

3 Use the Save Options radio buttons to specify what you want saved: only the active workbook or all the open workbooks.

4 Mark the Prompt Before Saving check box if you want Excel to display a message box prior to the automatic save.

Responding to AutoSave Prompt Messages

If you tell Excel it should prompt you before an automatic file save operation, it displays a message box like the one shown below to ask whether you really want to save the workbooks.

Select Save if you do want to save the workbooks.

Select Skip if you don't want to save the workbooks.

 **Saving Workbooks**

Check the check mark

Excel places a check mark in front of the Tools AutoSave command if automatic file saving is already turned on.

AutoSum

An autosum is simply a SUM() function you add with the AutoSum tool.

Using the AutoSum Tool

Select the row, column, or range you want to sum and then select the AutoSum tool.

Include an empty cell below each column you want to sum and to the right of each row you want to sum. Excel uses these empty cells for the new SUM() functions.

	A	B	C	D	E	F
1		January	February	March	Total	
2	Advertising	3990	570	890	5450	
3	Equipment	2330	3180	4080	9590	
4	Office	3840	3310	1770	8920	
5	Subcontractors	4300	1830	4320	10450	
6	Total	14460	8890	11060	34410	
7						
8						

Excel adds the SUM() functions to tally selected rows and columns. For example, in this cell, AutoSum adds the function,
=SUM(B2:D2)

Editing AutoSum Functions

You edit AutoSum functions in the same way you edit other formulas.

∴ Function Wizard; Math Functions

Bold Characters

You can **bold** characters in the current worksheet selection by pressing Ctrl+B or clicking the Bold Formatting toolbar button. You can also use the Format Cell command and its Font tab options.

∴ Changing Fonts

Boolean Algebra

Boolean algebra compares two values in a test question to determine if the question is true or is false. Sure, this may sound like something you don't want to get mixed up with, but Boolean algebra is very handy. You use Boolean algebraic expressions in conditional functions and in list filtering.

continues

Boolean Algebra *(continued)*

A1=B1	Is value in A1 equal to value in B1?
A1>B1	Is value in A1 greater than value in B1?
A1>=B1	Is value in A1 greater than or equal to value in B1?
A1<B1	Is value in A1 less than value in B1?
A1<=B1	Is value in A1 less than or equal to value in B1?
A1<>B1	Is value in A1 not equal to the value in B1?

 Conditional Functions; Formulas

The problem of precedence

The comparison operators used in a Boolean expression have lower precedence than the other arithmetic operations—such as exponentiation, multiplication and division, and addition and subtraction. In other words, the comparison calculation is the last calculation made in a formula that uses a Boolean expression.

Borders You can add border lines to cells. To do so, follow these steps:

1 Select the cell or cells.

2 Choose the Format Cells command. Excel displays the Format Cells dialog box.

3 Select the Border tab. Excel displays the Border options.

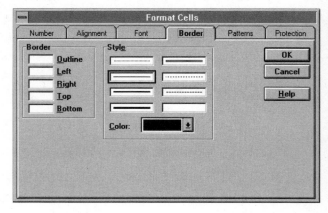

Borders *(continued)*

4 Use the Border buttons to choose on which cell edges the border should appear. Outline means around the outside edge of the cell selection, Left and Right means along the left and right edges of every selected cell, Top and Bottom, well, you can guess this, right?

5 Use the Style buttons to choose border line thickness and make other line style decisions, for example, choosing dashes.

6 Use the Color drop-down list to select a border line color if you want something other than basic black.

❖ **AutoFormatting Tables**

Calculating Formulas Excel is very clever about the way it calculates **formulas.** Very clever indeed. It recognizes dependencies—so if one formula uses another formula's result, this other, dependent formula gets calculated first. Here's another clever twist. Unless you direct Excel to do otherwise, Excel recalculates your formulas whenever a formula or an input changes. (You won't always be able to tell when Excel recalculates because it does so very quickly and in the background.)

If Excel is still recalculating a worksheet or if it needs to recalculate a worksheet, the word Calculate appears on the status bar. You can press F9 to manually tell Excel to recalculate.

Cell Address A cell address identifies a specific cell by giving the cell's location using the column letter and row number. The cell address I81, for example, identifies the cell at the intersection of column I and row 81. U812 identifies the cell at the intersection of column U and row 812.

continues

Cell Address *(continued)*

Cell addresses are mainly handy because you can use them in **formulas**. When you use a cell address in a formula, Excel retrieves the value stored in the cell and uses this value in the formula.

If you want to refer to a cell on another worksheet in the workbook, you need to precede the cell address with the sheet name and an exclamation point. Sheet2!B52, for example, identifies the cell at the intersection of column B and row 52 on Sheet2 of the workbook.

Cell Pointer Cell pointer is simply another name for the **cell selector**—that dark outline that marks the **active cell** and moves around the worksheet as you fiddle with the direction keys.

Cell Protection Adding cell protection to a workbook hides cell contents and prevents changes to the cell contents. Adding cell protection requires two actions. First, you need to tell Excel which cells it should protect and how it should protect them. Second, you need to tell Excel to turn on this protection.

Specifying Protected Cells

To tell Excel which cells it should protect and how it should protect them, follow these steps:

1 Select the cells.

2 Choose the Format Cells command.

3 Select the Protection tab.

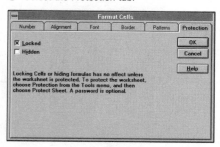

4 Mark the Locked check box to prevent changes to cell contents.

5 Mark the Hidden check box to prevent users from viewing cell contents on the formula bar. (The worksheet shows labels, values, and formula results; so do this to prevent users from viewing your formulas.)

Protecting a Worksheet

To turn on the protection in only the active worksheet, follow these steps:

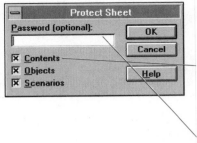

1 Choose the Tools Protection command.

2 Choose the Protect Sheet command.

3 Use the Contents, Objects, and Scenarios check boxes to specify what you want to protect.

4 If you want, add a protection password.

Unprotecting a Worksheet

To turn off cell protection, all someone needs to do is choose the Tools Protection Unprotect Sheet command. If you add a password, however, Excel will ask for the password before executing the command.

Protecting a Workbook

To turn on protection in all of a workbook's sheets, follow these steps:

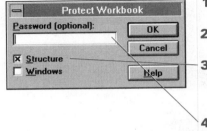

1 Choose the Tools Protection command.

2 Choose the Protect Workbook command.

3 Use the Structure and Windows check boxes to specify what you want to protect.

4 If you want, add a protection password.

continues

29

Cell Protection *(continued)*

Unprotecting a Workbook

To turn off cell protection, choose the Tools Protection Unprotect Workbook command. If you add a password, however, Excel will ask for the protection password before executing the command.

⁖ Passwords

Cell Reference
Cell reference is simply another name for **cell address**. I could, therefore, repeat the cell address definition given earlier, but let's save space instead. There are lots of cooler things to talk about.

⁖ Active Cell

Cell Selector
The cell selector is the square that Excel uses to mark the **active cell.** If you're confused by this, start Excel and look at your screen. Now fool around with the direction keys. See that thing that moves? That's the cell selector.

Changing Fonts
To change the **font** used for the selected cells' characters or the selected portion of text if you're editing a cell's contents, use the Format Cell command and the Font tab.

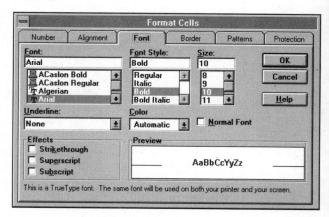

1 From the Font list box, select a font. Excel identifies printer fonts with the printer icon and identifies TrueType fonts with the **T** logo.

2 In the Font Style list box, indicate whether you want regular characters, bold characters, or italic characters.

3 In the Size list box, select a point size. (One point equals 1/72 inch.)

4 Use the Underline drop-down list box to add underlining. Use the Effects check boxes to specify other character effects such as subscript.

5 Add color using the Color drop-down list box. (Automatic means the Windows Control Panel controls color.)

6 Experiment with your font changes and then see their effect in the Sample box.

7 To return to the default, or suggested, font settings, mark the Normal Font check box. When you do, Excel sets the Font to Arial, the Font Style to Regular, the Size to 10, and the Color to Automatic. Excel also removes any underlining as well as any other special effects.

Making room for big characters

If you choose a larger point size, you may need to increase the row height to see the characters clearly.

Chart A chart is a picture that visually depicts worksheet data. In Excel you create these pictures-worth-a-thousand-words with the **ChartWizard.**

Chart Types

Chart Colors You can change the color of most parts of a chart—if the chart menu bar is displayed because the chart appears on a separate sheet or if you double-clicked an embedded chart.

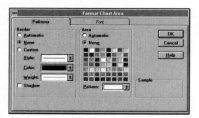

Changing Chart Part Colors

1 Select the part you want to change—by clicking, for example.

2 Choose the Format Selected Series/Selected Object command. (The command the Format menu shows depends on the chart part you select.)

3 Select the Patterns tab. The Patterns tab options provide settings you can use to change the selected chart part's colors.

4 In the Border Color drop-down list box, select a color for the line drawn around the edge of the chart part—if the chart part has a border line.

5 In the Area colors options box, select the background color for the chart part.

❖ Editing Embedded Charts

I just want that one

To select a single **data marker** rather than all the data markers in the series, press Ctrl and then click the data marker.

Chart Gridlines

You can use chart gridlines to make it easier to calibrate the values plotted in a chart and to differentiate the categories.

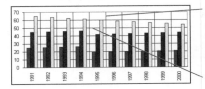

Category axis gridlines extend perpendicularly from the category axis—and help you keep the data categories straight.

Value axis gridlines extend perpendicularly from the value axis—and help you more easily calibrate plotted values.

Adding Value Axis Gridlines

To add value axis gridlines to a chart, select the Gridlines tool.

Adding Value and Category Axis Gridlines

To add both value axis and category axis gridlines, choose the Insert Gridlines command.

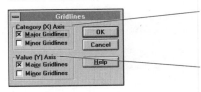

1 Use the Category (X) Axis check boxes to add or remove category axis gridlines.

2 Use the Value (Y) Axis check boxes to add or remove value axis gridlines.

Distinguishing between major and minor gridlines

Major gridlines extend from all the major tickmarks. Minor gridlines extend from all the minor tickmarks. Tickmarks are those little lines, or dashes, that intersect the axis.

Chart Legends

You use chart legends to name the **data series** plotted in a chart. Assuming you were either lucky or astute enough to include the data series names in your chart data selection, you can add a chart legend by clicking the Chart toolbar's Legend tool.

continues

Chart Legends *(continued)*

Unfortunately, if you don't include the data series names in your chart data selection, Excel doesn't know what to name the series. So it simply uses names such as Series1, Series2, and so on. Pretty boring, right? For this reason, it's a good idea to include data series names in your chart data selection.

❖ **ChartWizard; Data Categories**

Chart Page Setup
Choose the File Page Setup command and choose the Chart tab to display a dialog box you'll use to specify how charts print. (For this tab to appear, the active sheet must display a chart. If this chart is embedded, first double-click the chart to select it.)

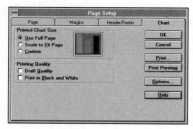

Changing the Chart Size

Use the Printed Chart Size radio buttons to control size. Mark Use Full Page if Excel should size the chart so that it uses the entire page. Mark Scale to Fit Page if Excel should print the chart so that it's as large as will fit on the page but still uses the same ratio of height to width as the chart on your screen. Mark Custom if you want to print the chart using the on-screen dimensions.

Changing the Print Quality

Mark the Draft Quality check box to indicate that you want Excel to print faster at a lower resolution. Mark the Print in Black and White check box if you want Excel to print in black even though your printer outputs color.

❖ **Printing**

Chart Sheets Excel charts appear either as objects embedded in a worksheet or as separate workbook sheets. When you use the **ChartWizard** tool or the Insert Chart On This Sheet command to create a new chart, Excel embeds a chart object in the active worksheet. But you can place the chart on its own sheet by selecting the chart and using the Insert Chart As New Sheet command.

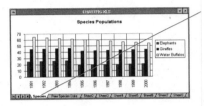

When you use the Insert Chart As New Sheet command, Excel places the chart on a new sheet.

Chart Text You can annotate charts by adding text.

Adding Chart Text

To add text to a chart, display the chart's sheet or double-click the embedded chart, press Esc to be sure that nothing is selected, and then begin typing. To separate the text into separate lines, press Ctrl+Enter at the point where you want a line to end. Excel places your text in roughly the middle of the chart's plot area. You can move the text by dragging.

Formatting chart text

You can format chart text and **chart titles** in the same ways that you format cell contents. To format chart text, select the text and then choose the Format Selected Object command. To format chart titles, select the title and then choose the Format Selected Chart Title command.

Chart Titles You can add text to charts that titles the chart and describe the axes. The easiest way to do this is to use the **ChartWizard.** With the ChartWizard, you can add chart titles when you create the chart, or you can modify an existing chart. To modify an existing chart, display the chart's sheet if it has its own sheet or select the chart if it's embedded, and then click the ChartWizard tool.

A chart title appears above the chart—and usually describes the chart's visual message or summarizes the data.

Axis titles appear next to the horizontal and vertical axes and describe what's being plotted.

Using different fonts in the same chart text

Look closely at the category title in the preceding chart and you'll see that the first line is in **bold** and that the second line is in *italic.* To format a chunk of title or text differently, select a portion of the text and use the Format Selected Text/Selected Title command.

Chart Types Excel supplies 14 chart types. You can choose a chart type when you create the chart, and you can change the selected chart's type using the Format Chart Type command. Which method you use depends on the visual comparison you want.

Type	What chart shows
Area	**Area charts** plot data series as cumulative lines. The first data series values are plotted in a line. Then the second data series values are plotted in a line that gets stacked on top of the first line. Then the third data series values get stacked on top of the second line, and so on.

Type	What chart shows

 A **Bar chart** plots each data series values using horizontal bars. Good for comparing individual values when the chart data category isn't time.

 A **Column chart** is like a bar chart, but it plots each data series values as vertical bars. Good for comparing individual values when the chart data category is time.

 A **Line chart** plots each data series values as points on a line. Emphasizes trends in the data series values.

 A **Pie chart** plots a single data series with each value in the series represented as a pie slice. Probably the least effective chart type available because you're technically limited to a single data series and practically limited to a small number of values. (Otherwise you slice the pie into too many pieces.)

 A **Doughnut chart** plots data series in rings, with each value in the series represented as a segment (bite) of the ring (doughnut).

 Radar charts plot data series values using a separate value axis for each category. Value axes radiate from the center of the chart.

 An **XY, or Scatter, chart** uses two value axes gridlines to plot pairs of data points in a line. Because it visually shows the correlation between two data series, this is the most powerful and useful chart type available.

continues

Chart Types *(continued)*

Type	What chart shows
3-D Area	Like its two-dimensional cousin, the **3-D Area chart** plots data series with lines and then colors the area between the lines. Note that some of the 3-D area chart autoformats use the third dimension of depth to organize the data series.
3-D Bar	A **3-D Bar chart** plots each data series values using horizontal solid bars. Good for comparing individual values when the chart category isn't time—but a bit imprecise.
3-D Column	A **3-D Column chart** plots each data series values as solid vertical bars. Note that some of the 3-D column chart autoformats use the third dimension of depth to organize the data series. Like the 3-D bar chart, a bit imprecise.
3-D Line	A **3-D Line chart** should probably be called a ribbon chart. It plots each data series values as points on a ribbon. Emphasizes trends in the data series values, but tricky to use. (The ribbon's three-dimensionality makes it difficult to accurately gauge how fast the line rises or falls.)
3-D Pie	A **3-D Pie chart** plots a single data series with each value in the series represented as a pie wedge in a solid cylinder. Extremely difficult to use well. (Pie wedges in the chart background appear smaller than same-sized pie wedges in the foreground.)
3-D Surface	A **3-D Surface chart** plots data series as lines in a three-dimensional grid and then colors the surface between the data series. Often useful for creating rectangular data maps. (A data map plots values on a map using latitudinal and longitudinal coordinates.)

C

ChartWizard Excel's ChartWizard creates charts that visually depict

workbook data. To use the ChartWizard, select the data
you want to plot.(In your selection, include the data series
names. Be sure to include the category names too if they
appear in the worksheet.) Then follow these steps:

1 Click the ChartWizard tool. Excel changes the mouse pointer to a
cross-hair. (That's right—just like the cross-hair a hunter sees
through a rifle scope.)

2 Draw the box in which you want to place the chart. To do this,
click on the upper left corner of the box, drag the mouse to the
lower right corner, and then release the mouse button. Excel displays the first ChartWizard dialog box.

3 Confirm your chart data selection and then select Next. Excel displays the second ChartWizard dialog box. (You can use the Back
and Next buttons to move between ChartWizard dialog boxes.)

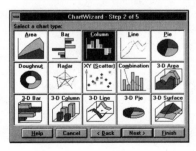

continues

ChartWizard (continued)

4 In the second ChartWizard dialog box, select a chart type by clicking its box. Select Next. Excel displays the third ChartWizard dialog box.

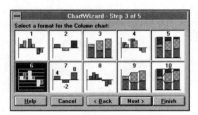

5 Select one of the chart styles, or autoformats, available for the chart type. Select Next. Excel displays the fourth ChartWizard dialog box.

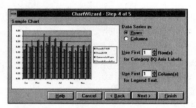

6 Indicate whether you arranged your data series by rows or by columns.

7 Indicate which row holds the category names. (Excel knows whether your category names are in a column or a row by looking at the way you've arranged your data series. So this option's name changes depending on the way you've arranged your data series.)

8 Indicate which column holds the data series names. (Excel knows whether your data series names are in a row or a column by looking at the way you've arranged your data series too. So this option's name changes depending on the way you've arranged your data series.) Select Next. Excel displays the fifth (and final!) ChartWizard dialog box.

9 Indicate whether you want Excel to add a legend that names the data series and identifies their data markers. Excel places the legend to the right of the chart.

10 Type the text you want to appear above the chart. Type text you want to appear next to the categories axis or values axis. Then select Finish.

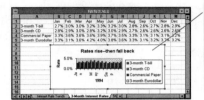

Excel embeds a chart like the one you've described in the active worksheet. An embedded chart floats, or sits on top of, the worksheet holding the plotted data.

⁘ Environment: Microsoft Excel Charts

Clip Art

Clip art refers to the graphic images you can paste into documents. Although Excel doesn't come with any clip art, Microsoft Word for Windows does. (If you acquired Excel as part of purchasing Microsoft Office, you have Word for Windows and its clip art.) You can place clip art images into Excel workbooks as either pictures or objects.

⁘ Object Linking and Embedding; Worksheet Pictures

Clipboard

Ever see the television show "Star Trek"? If you did, you may remember the transporter room. It let the *Starship Enterprise* move Captain Kirk, Mr. Spock, and just about anything else just about anywhere. The Clipboard is the Windows equivalent of the *Enterprise*'s transporter room.

With the Clipboard, Windows easily moves just about anything anywhere. In Excel, you can use the Clipboard to move chunks of text, values, worksheet ranges, and even graphic images to and from different files. You can also use the Clipboard to move text, worksheet ranges, and even graphic images between Excel and other Windows applications such as Microsoft Word for Windows.

continues

Clipboard *(continued)*

Using the Clipboard

To move information around via the Clipboard, you actually use the Edit menu's Cut, Copy, Paste, and Paste Special commands. So you don't have to know all that much about the Clipboard to make good use of it. One thing you should remember about the Clipboard, however, is that it stores what you've copied or cut temporarily. After you copy or cut, the next time you do so, the previous Clipboard contents are replaced. And when you exit Windows, the Clipboard contents are erased.

∴ Object Linking and Embedding

Closing Workbooks
You close **workbooks** so that they don't consume memory, so that they don't clutter your screen, and so that they don't just plain annoy you.

Closing a Single Workbook

To close a workbook, double-click its Control-menu box, or be sure the window is active and then choose the File Close command.

Closing All Workbooks

To close all the open workbook windows at once, hold down Shift and then choose the File Close All command.

So you don't lose changes

If you've made changes to the workbook and haven't yet saved it, Excel asks if you first want to save.

Color
You can change the color of most parts of worksheets and charts.

Changing cell background colors—**Patterns**	
Changing the color of labels and values—**Fonts**	
Changing the color of border lines—**Borders**	
Changing colors in a chart—**Chart Colors**	

Coloring Worksheet Ranges You can color the selected
worksheet range using the Formatting toolbar's Color
button.

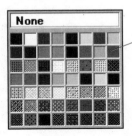

Click the down arrow
next to the Color toolbar
button; then select one
of the colors from the
palette box that Excel
provides.

∴ **Coloring Worksheet Text; Formatting**

Coloring Worksheet Text You can color the characters in,
the selected worksheet range using the Formatting
toolbar's Font Color button.

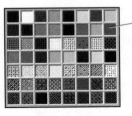

Click the down arrow
next to the Font Color
button; then select one
of the colors from the
palette box that Excel
provides.

∴ **Coloring Worksheet Ranges; Formatting**

Columns You can change the width of columns with the mouse
or with the Format Columns submenu commands, but
using the mouse is easier. To change the width of a selected column or of several selected columns with the
mouse, drag the edge of the column letter label.

continues

43

Columns *(continued)*

Drag the edge of the column letter label left or right to change a column's width. Excel changes the mouse pointer to a two-directional arrow when you position the mouse on the column edge.

❖ **Rows**

Conditional Functions
Conditional functions perform a logical test (described using **Boolean algebra**) and return a value or text string based on the results of the test.

Suppose, for example, that you're a teacher and that you want a formula that compares a student's final test score, the value in the cell named TestScore, with 60. If the student's test score equals or exceeds this value, the student passes. Otherwise, well, you get the picture. Here is an example conditional IF function.

=IF(TestScore>=60,"P","F")

This IF function compares the value in the cell named TestScore with 60. If the value in TestScore equals or exceeds 60, the function returns the one-character string P. If the value in TestScore is less than 60, the function returns the one-character string F.

❖ **Argument; Function Wizard**

Converting Formulas into Numbers
If you want to convert a formula to the value it returns, select the cell with the formula, choose Edit Copy, choose Edit Paste Special, mark the Paste Values radio button, and select OK. If you want to convert the **formulas** in a worksheet range to **values,** simply select the range with the formulas and then choose the Edit Copy and Edit Paste Special commands.

Copying You can copy and paste **values, labels,** formats, worksheet selections, and even graphic objects. You can do so within Excel or between Excel and another Windows application.

Copying Cell Formats You can reuse the format of one cell for other cells.

Using the Format Painter Tool

One way—and often the easiest way—to copy formats is with the Format Painter tool. To do this, follow these steps:

1 Select a cell with the formatting that you want to reuse.

2 Click the Format Painter tool.

3 Select the cells you want to format and press Enter.

Copying Formats with Commands

You can also copy cell formats by taking these steps:

1 Select the cell with the format you want to copy.

2 Choose Edit Copy.

3 Select the cell or cells in which you want to use the format.

4 Choose Edit Paste Special.

continues

Copying Cell Formats *(continued)*

5 When Excel displays the Paste Special dialog box, mark the Paste Formats radio button and then select OK.

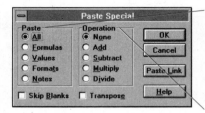

The Paste Special's Paste radio buttons let you control which features you've assigned to the cell get pasted into other cells and reused.

The Paste Special's Operation radio buttons let you specify whether pasted values should be combined in some way with the values already in the cells. You leave this set as None if you're pasting cell formats.

Copying Data   You can copy **values** and **labels** between cells using the mouse or commands.

Copying with the Mouse

To use the mouse, follow these steps:

1 Select the cell.

2 Drag the selected cell's border to its new location.

Copying with Commands

To use the Edit Copy and Edit Paste commands, follow these steps:

1 Select the cell with the value or the label.

2 Choose Edit Copy.

3 Select the cell to which you want to copy the value or the label.

4 Choose Edit Paste.

⠶ **Clipboard; Copying Ranges; Drag-and-Drop; Moving Data**

C

Copying Formulas You can copy formulas between cells. The way you do this, however, depends on whether you want Excel to adjust any **relative cell addresses** used in the formula.

When Excel Should Adjust Formulas

If you want Excel to adjust the formula's relative cell addresses, take the following steps:

1 Select the cell with the formula.

2 Choose Edit Copy.

3 Select the cell to which you want to copy the formula.

4 Choose Edit Paste.

	A	B	C	D
1		**Actual**	**Budget**	
2	2x4s	35.67	40	
3	Plywood	76.42	80	
4	Nails	1.95	2	
5	**Total**	114.04		
6				
7				

This formula,=B2+B3+B4, adds the values in the cells above it.

Rather than reenter the same basic formula into cell C5, you can copy the formula in cell B5 to cell C5. Because the formula in B5 uses relative cell addresses, Excel pastes the formula =C2+C3+C4 into cell C5.

When Excel Shouldn't Adjust Formulas

If you don't want Excel to adjust the relative cell addresses used in the formula, you can make these relative cell addresses absolute (by editing the formula), or you can follow these steps:

1 Select the cell with the formula.

2 Click the formula bar and then select the formula.

3 Choose Edit Copy.

4 Select the cell to which you want to copy the formula.

5 Choose Edit Paste.

⁂ Copying Data; Moving Data

Copying Objects and Pictures

To copy worksheet objects and pictures you've inserted, simply follow these steps:

1 Select the object or picture. Excel adds selection handles.

2 Choose Edit Copy.

3 Click the cell over which the object's upper left corner should float.

4 Choose Edit Paste.

 Moving Objects and Pictures; Resizing Pictures; Worksheet Pictures

Copying Ranges

You can use either the Edit Copy and Edit Paste commands or the mouse to copy a range.

Copying with Commands

To copy a worksheet range (and the **labels, values,** and **formulas** it holds) with the Edit Copy and Edit Paste commands, follow these steps:

1 Select the cells you want to copy by dragging the mouse between the opposite corners of the worksheet range. Excel highlights the range to indicate it's been selected.

2 Choose Edit Copy.

3 Select the upper-left corner of the range into which the copied cells should be placed.

4 Choose Edit Paste.

Copying with the Mouse

To copy a worksheet range with the mouse, follow these steps:

1 Select the cells you want to copy.

2 Hold down Ctrl.

3 Click on the edge of the range.

4 Drag the selected range to the new location.

 Moving Data

Automatic formula adjustments

When you copy a worksheet range, Excel adjusts the relative cell addresses used by any of the copied formulas.

Copying Sheets ❖ Moving and Copying Sheets

Creating Lists To create a list on a worksheet, follow these steps:

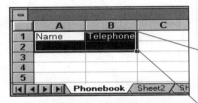

1 Name the worksheet (preferably, something clever).

2 Enter the column headers, or field names, in the first worksheet row.

3 Select the header row and the next empty row.

4 Choose the Data Form command.

5 Fill in the text boxes.

6 Select New to add an entry to the list.

7 Repeat steps 5 and 6 for every list entry you want to add—or until you want a break because you're tired.

❖ List Management

49

Currency Symbols

Excel uses a currency symbol to punctuate monetary values that you format as currency. Which currency symbol Excel uses depends on the Control Panel's International settings.

Changing Currency Symbols

To change the currency symbol Excel uses, start the Control Panel, display the International settings (for example, by selecting the Settings International command), select the Change Currency Format command button, and then enter a new currency symbol in the Symbol text box.

About Control Panel changes

Control Panel changes you make—for example, to the currency symbol—won't take effect until the next time you start Windows.

ANSI Characters; Formatting Numbers

Custom Filtering

The Data Filter command provides two methods for filtering lists. Often the quicker and easier method is to use the Data Filter AutoFilter command. You can also use the Data Filter Advanced command—if you're adventurous. Or if you're clever enough to figure out how the command works without help from me.

Filtering Lists

Databases ⁙ List Management

Data Categories Data categories organize the values in a chart's **data series.** This sounds confusing, but let me give you an easy rule of thumb. In any chart that shows how some value changes over time, data categories are time periods. So in a chart that plots sales over a 5-year period—say, 1991 to 1995—it's the years that are the data categories.

Data Markers Data markers are the visual building blocks that Excel uses to draw a chart. Each Excel **chart type** uses a different data marker. A column chart, for example, has column data markers. A pie chart has pie-slice data markers. A line chart uses—no, wait a minute. You now know a line chart uses lines as data markers, right? One thing you may not know but may find interesting is that Excel also lets you use pictures as data markers.

⁙ **Picture Charts**

Data Series A data series is simply a set of related values plotted with the same **data marker** in an Excel chart. If you find the term *data series* confusing, you can use a sneaky trick to identify the data series that a chart plots. Ask yourself, "What am I plotting?" Every one-word answer will identify a data series. For example, if you ask the "What am I plotting?" question about a chart that plots sales revenue over 5 years, you can answer, "Sales." Sales then is a data series. By the way, the data markers that visually represent the sales set of values will all look similar. For example, the sales data series might be depicted with a set of red bars or as points along the same line.

⁙ **Data Categories**

Date Formats

Excel provides a whole slew of date formats that you can use to make **date values** understandable.

Date Format Codes

Here's a list of the ways Excel lets you format an example date value, 35000:

Format code	Formatted date value
m/d/yy	10/28/95
d-mmm-yy	28-Oct-95
d-mmm	28-Oct
mmm-yy	Oct-95
m/d/y h:mm	10/28/95 12:00a

Formatting a Date

To format a date, select the cell or range with the date values. Then choose the Format Cells command and select the Date entry from the Category list. Finally, choose one of the date format entries from the Format Codes list box.

 Formatting Numbers; Time Values

Date and Time Functions

Excel provides more than a dozen functions to make working with **date values** and **time values** easier. Using the DATE function, for example, you can easily determine the date value for a particular day. The function below returns the date value for December 31, 1995, which is 35064, by using as function arguments the year number (1995), the month number (12), and the day number (31):

=DATE(1995,12,31)

 Argument; Function Wizard

Date Values Excel lets you use values to represent dates: 1 to represent January 1, 1900, 2 to represent January 2, 1900, and so on, through 65390 to represent December 31, 2078. You of course don't want to have to remember which date the value 40000 represents; so Excel formats date values so that they look like dates.

This may all seem like much ado about nothing, but you can do some neat tricks with date values. Say, you've got a workbook that keeps a record of invoices and estimates payment dates. If an invoice is due 30 days from the invoice date—for example, October 28, 1995—you can calculate the invoice due date by adding the value 30 to the date value for October 28, 1995 (35000). The formula result, 35030, gives the day you should expect payment. Of course, 35030 doesn't mean a whole heck of a lot to you or to me, but once you tell Excel to format this as November 27, 1995, things begin to look pretty clear.

∴ **Date Formats; Formulas; Time Values**

Moving worksheets to the Apple Macintosh

If you move Excel workbooks between Windows and the Apple Macintosh, be fore-warned: Excel for the Macintosh uses a different date value numbering scheme. On the Macintosh, the value 1 represents January 2, 1904. (If you want Excel for Win-dows to use the same date value numbering scheme as Excel for the Macintosh, choose the Tools Options command, select the Calculation tab, and mark the 1904 Date System check box.)

Default Directory If you want Excel to suggest a default direc-tory for the workbooks you save, follow these steps:

1 Choose the Tools Op-tions command.

2 Select the General tab.

3 Enter the path name for the directory in the Default File Location text box.

4 Select OK.

∴ **Saving Workbooks**

Default Fonts

Microsoft Excel, by default, uses 10-point Arial type for worksheets. To use another font, follow these steps:

1 Choose the Tools Options command.
2 Select the General tab.
3 Select the font from the Standard Font drop-down list box.
4 Select the point size from the Size drop-down list box.
5 Select OK. The next time you start Excel, your new font style and size setting will be used for new worksheets.

Default Workbooks

Want a particular workbook to load every single time you start Excel? No problem. All you need to do is save the workbook in the XLSTART subdirectory of the EXCEL directory.

☆ **Saving Workbooks**

Deleting

You can remove, or delete, cells, charts, columns, rows, and worksheets.

Removing cells—**Deleting Cells**
Removing charts—**Deleting Sheets**
Removing columns—**Deleting Columns and Rows**
Removing rows—**Deleting Columns and Rows**
Removing worksheets—**Deleting Sheets**

Deleting versus erasing

When you delete a cell, column, or row, it no longer exists in the worksheet. In other words, Excel physically removes the cell, column, or row and then rearranges the worksheet so that there are no empty holes, or gaps. In comparison, when you clear, or erase, a cell, column, or row, Excel removes only the cell's contents and formatting.

Deleting Cells To delete, or remove, cells from a row or a column, select the cells and then choose the Edit Delete command.

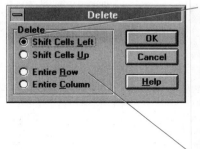

Use the Delete radio buttons to tell Excel how it should fill the "hole" left after the deletion: by moving up the cells in the selected column (indicated as Shift Cells Up) or by moving left the cells in the selected row (indicated as Shift Cells Left).

Don't use the Entire Row or Entire Column radio buttons unless you want to delete the selected cells' rows or columns.

∴ **Deleting Columns and Rows**

Deleting Columns and Rows To delete columns or rows from a worksheet, select the columns or rows and then choose the Edit Delete command.

∴ **Deleting Cells; Editing Cell Contents; Error Messages**

Deleting List Entries ∴ **Editing Lists**

Deleting Sheets To delete a **worksheet** or a **chart sheet**, display the sheet and then choose the Edit Delete Sheet command.

Delimited Text Files A delimited text file is a file that uses a standard character—for example, the Tab character—to break apart the lines, or rows, of information. Excel's File Open command starts a wizard that helps you import text files including delimited text files.

> ❖ **ASCII Text Files; Importing Text Files**

Dependents A dependent is a cell with a formula that references, or addresses, other cells. For example, if cell A1 uses the formula =B12+E6, it uses the values in cells B12 or E6. Cell A1, then, is a dependent cell (it "depends on") of cells B12 and E6.

> ❖ **Auditing Worksheets; Precedents**

Dialog Box A dialog box is simply an on-screen form you fill out to tell Excel how to complete a command. Any command name followed by ellipses (...) displays a dialog box.

Document Window The document window is the rectangle that Excel uses to display your workbooks. If you have more than one workbook open, the **application window** will show more than one document window.

Counting the open document windows

The Window menu lists numbered commands for all of the open document windows. By activating the Window menu, you can learn how many and which document windows are open.

Drag-and-Drop

Drag-and-drop is a technique that lets you move and copy pieces of a workbook with the mouse.

Moving with Drag-and-Drop

To move some piece of a workbook—such as a cell, a range, or a picture—you select it and then drag it to its new location.

Copying with Drag-and-Drop

To copy some piece of a workbook—such as a cell, a range, or a picture—you select it, press Ctrl, and then drag it to its new location.

Copying; Moving Data

Drop-and-Drag

I think this is the name of a TV show about hunting. It's on one of the cable stations. I mention this only so you don't confuse the TV show with the similarly named Excel feature, **Drag-and-Drop**.

Drawing

Use the Drawing tool, which appears on the standard Excel toolbar, to draw objects such as arrows, circles, and rectangles by dragging the mouse. Select the Drawing tool to activate the Drawing toolbar.

Once the Drawing toolbar appears, select one of the Drawing tools on the first row of toolbar buttons and then drag the mouse to whatever shows on the button's face—in this case, an arrow.

The second row of toolbar buttons provides command shortcuts for working with graphic objects.

Moving Objects and Pictures

Editing Cell Contents To change the formula, value, or text stored in a cell, replace the cell's contents by entering some new formula, value, or piece of text into the cell. Or double-click the cell so that Excel turns the cell into an editable text box. (That's "editable," not "edible.") Now make your changes.

You can also use the formula bar to edit the **active cell.** Simply click the formula bar, and Excel adds three buttons related to editing the formula bar.

The formula bar shows the contents of the selected cell—in this case, a simple formula. It works like an editable text box.

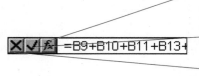

You start the **FunctionWizard** by selecting this button.

When you finish, click the OK button.

If you don't want to move the edited contents shown on the formula bar to the cell, click the Cancel button.

Editing Embedded Charts If you want to edit an embedded chart, double-click it. From the Chart menu bar, use the Insert and Format menus to make additions, changes, and other what-have-yous. When you finish editing the chart, press Esc to redisplay the regular work sheet menu bar, or select a worksheet cell.

Chart Colors; ChartWizard

Editing Lists To edit a list, select the list (including the headers) and then choose the Data Form command. Make your changes in the Data Form dialog box.

1 Use the scroll bar to display the list entry you want to change. (You can also use the PageUp and PageDown keys to move through the list.)

2 When the list entry is displayed, edit the text box contents.

3 Select Restore to undo your changes.

4 To delete the list entry shown in the dialog box, select Delete.

❖ **Creating Lists; List Management; Searching Lists**

More about Restore

To reverse editing changes you've made to the list entry currently displayed, select Restore. Note, though, that you must select Restore before displaying another list entry. Also, Restore won't restore a list entry you've previously deleted.

Embedding and Linking Existing Objects
To create an object using an existing file, follow these steps:

1 Choose the Insert Object command.

2 Select the Create from File tab.

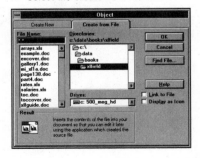

3 Use the Directories and Drives list boxes to find the object file. (Or select the Find File button to select the File Find File command.)

continues

Embedding and Linking Existing Objects *(continued)*

4 Use the File Name list box to identify the object file.

5 Mark the Link to File check box if you want Windows to update the object for subsequent file changes.

6 Mark the Display as Icon check box if you want Excel to display an icon to represent the embedded object rather than a picture of the embedded object.

7 Select OK when you finish describing the embedded or linked object. Excel embeds an object into your Excel Worksheet.

❖ **Copying Objects and Pictures; Moving Objects and Pictures; Resizing Pictures; Worksheet Pictures**

Embedding New Objects
To create an object from scratch using an application other than Excel, follow these steps:

1 Choose the Insert Object command.

2 Select the Create New tab.

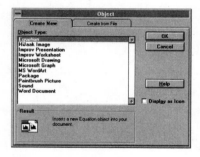

3 Use the Object Type list box to select the Windows application you'll use to create the object you are about to embed.

4 Mark the Display as Icon check box if you want to see the embedded object as an icon rather than a picture of the embedded object.

5 When you select OK, Excel starts the selected application so that you can create the object. (To see the object in your Excel worksheet, use the selected application's File Update command.)

🐾 **Embedding and Linking Existing Objects**

Entering Data To enter a value or a piece of text in a cell, simply click the cell and then type whatever you want stored in the cell. You can enter **values, labels** (pieces of text), or **formulas** in this way.

Predictable patterns

If you want to enter values that follow a predictable pattern, choose the Edit Fill Series command. What's a predictable pattern? Good question. Here are a couple of examples: a series of month-end date values, a set of numbers that increase by a set value (such as 1) or by a set percentage (such as 5%).

Erasing Cells You can erase cell contents, formatting, and notes using the Edit Clear submenu commands.

Erasing a Cell's Contents

To erase cell contents (meaning the stuff—values, labels, or formulas—stored in the cell), choose the Edit Clear Contents command or press Del.

Erasing Formatting

To erase formatting assigned to a cell, choose the Edit Clear Formats command.

Erasing Cell Notes

To erase notes attached to a cell, choose the Edit Clear Notes command.

continues

Erasing Cells *(continued)*

Erasing Cell Contents, Formatting, and Notes

If you want to wipe out everything associated with the cell—its contents, it formats, and its **notes**—choose the Edit Clear All command.

⁂ **Formatting**

The wrong way to erase

Don't remove a cell's contents with the spacebar. When you select a cell and then press the spacebar, you don't erase the cell's contents. You replace the cell contents with a space character.

Erasing Workbooks **Workbooks** are files stored on disk. To erase them, therefore, you use either the Windows File Manager application or the MS-DOS Del or Erase commands. For information about how to use the File Manager or MS-DOS to erase a workbook file, refer to the user documentation that came with your copy of Windows or MS-DOS.

If you accidentally erase a workbook

You should know that it may be possible to recover, or unerase, a workbook file. How you unerase files is beyond the scope of this little book, but if you've just erased a workbook that you now realize you desperately need, stop what you're doing. Don't save anything else to your hard disk. And look up the File Undelete command in the MS-DOS user documentation

Error Messages If a **formula** doesn't work right and Excel knows why, Excel will display one of the following messages:

Message	The problem is that your formula
#DIV/0	attempts the undefined operation of dividing by zero.
#NAME?	uses a cell name you haven't defined or one you've misspelled.

Message	The problem is that your formula
#VALUE!	tries to arithmetically manipulate something that's not a value—such as text.
#REF!	addresses a cell or a range that doesn't exist —perhaps because you deleted it.
#NULL	tries to return a value that doesn't exist.
#N/A	addresses a cell that holds the "not available" code, #N/A.
#NUM!	attempts some impossible mathematical operation such as calculating the root of a negative value.

Exiting Excel To exit from Excel—or just about any other Windows application—you can choose the File Exit command. Or you can close the Excel application window—for example, by double-clicking its Control-menu box. Excel will ask if you want to save workbooks with unsaved changes.

> **Closing Workbooks; Saving Workbooks; Windows Command Buttons**

Exporting Exporting is copying a workbook so that you or a friend can use it with another spreadsheet or word-processor application. You can export an Excel workbook by saving a workbook in a file format that the other program can use.

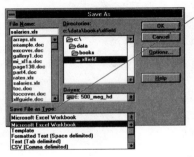

To export a workbook file, save the file in a format that the other program can open.

File Names
You give a workbook its file name when you choose the File Save As command.

Choosing a File Name

MS-DOS file-naming rules apply to Excel workbook files. A file name can't use more than eight characters. All numbers and letters that appear on your keyboard are OK. And so are many other characters. You can't, however, use characters that MS-DOS expects to be used in special ways on its command line, such as spaces, asterisks, and question marks. If you need more information than this, refer to the MS-DOS *User's Guide* that almost surely came with your computer.

Choosing a File Extension

The MS-DOS file extension, by the way, isn't something you need to worry about. Excel uses file extensions to identify file type. You can accept the default Microsoft Excel workbook file type, XLS, or you can use the File Save dialog box's File Type drop-down list box to select some other file type.

∴ Save Options; Saving Workbooks

File Summary
In addition to the worksheets and charts you store in workbook, you can store additional information that describes the workbook itself and makes it easier to find. You collect and store this additional information by filling out the Summary Info dialog box, which Excel displays any time you use the File Save As command to create a new workbook file.

In the Title text box, enter a title for your workbook.

Add keywords that will make it easy to later find the workbook file using the File Find File command.

Describe additional information about the workbook file using the Comments box.

Changing your mind

You can also edit the active workbook's summary information by choosing the File Summary Info command.

Filling Cells To fill a selected range with **formulas, values,** or **labels,** use one of the Edit Fill menu's commands.

Edit Fill Down

Choose the Edit Fill Down command to copy contents of the first, topmost row into the second and subsequent rows.

Edit Fill Right

Choose the Edit Fill Right command to copy contents of the first, leftmost column into second and subsequent columns.

Edit Fill Up

Choose the Edit Fill Up command to copy contents of the last, bottommost row into preceding rows.

Edit Fill Left

Choose the Edit Fill Left command to copy contents of the last, rightmost column into preceding columns.

Edit Fill Across Worksheets

Choose the Edit Fill Across Worksheets command to copy contents of the first workbook sheet into second and subsequent worksheets.

Edit Fill Justify

Choose the Edit Fill Justify command to rearrange the active cell's label so that it evenly fills the selected cells.

 Fill Series

Fill Series Sometimes you'll want to fill cells with a series of
values that fit a predictable pattern: only even numbers,
for example, or month-end dates. Excel provides a special command, Edit Fill Series, which lets you do just this.
To use the Edit Fill Series command, follow these steps:

1 Enter the series first value in the first cell of the range.

2 Select the cells you want to fill.

3 Choose the Edit Fill Series command. Excel displays the Series
dialog box.

4 Indicate whether the series should be filled a row at a time or a
column at a time.

5 Describe the pattern:

Pattern	Description
Linear	Create the pattern by adding the Step Value to the preceding cell's value.
Growth	Create the pattern by multiplying the Step Value by the preceding cell's value.
Date	Create a date-based pattern as described by the Step Value and Date Unit option.
AutoFill	Create a pattern based on the first cell's value. (AutoFill copies formulas, and it linearly adjusts values by the Step Value.)

6 Enter the Step Value used to create the pattern.

7 Optionally, enter the Stop Value that terminates the pattern.

Filtering Lists When you filter a list, you actually create a new list of entries that match a specified description.

Filtering an Existing List

1 Select the list.

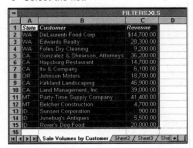

2 Choose the Data Filter AutoFilter command. Excel turns the header cells into drop-down list boxes.

3 Describe the list entries you want on your new list by activating the header drop-down list boxes and selecting a value. Or select one of the other entries such as All, Blanks, NonBlanks, or Custom.

4 If you select Custom, Excel displays the Custom AutoFilter dialog box.

5 Use the operator and value drop-down list boxes to create a **Boolean algebra** expression that describes the filter; for example, =CA tells Excel you want list entries that show the state as CA.

Filtering with wildcards

When you enter **values,** you can use the ? character to represent any single character. And you can use the * character to represent any group of characters. The filter State=C? would return any 2-character state code starting with the letter C. The filter Customer=B* would return any customer name starting with the letter B.

Filtering Lists *(continued)*

6 Create compound AND/OR filters by marking the AND/OR radio buttons and using the second set of operator and value drop-down list boxes.

	A	B	C	D
1	Sta	Customer	Revenue	
5	CA	Gonzalez & Shearson, Attorneys	36,200.00	
6	CA	Hapsburg Restaurant	14,700.00	
7	CA	Ito & Company	6,100.00	
9	CA	Kirkland Landscaping	46,900.00	
10	CA	Land Management, Inc	39,000.00	
16				
17				

7 After you specify the filter, select OK. Excel creates a new list of only those entries matching the filter.

Creating a New List from a Filtered List

To create a new list using the filtered list, copy the filtered list to a new worksheet location.

Displaying an Entire List Again

Choose the Data Filter Show All command to, in effect, unfilter a previously filtered list.

Removing the AutoFilter Drop-down List Boxes

Choose the Data Filter AutoFilter command. (Yes, again.)

Using Advanced Filters

The Data Filter menu's Advanced Filter displays a dialog box you use to identify the worksheet ranges holding the list and the filter descriptions (which need to be in the form of Boolean algebra expressions). I'm not going to describe this command here. Most people shouldn't ever need to use the Advanced Filter command.

⁂Creating Lists

Financial Functions Excel provides 15 financial functions for making depreciation expense calculations, for performing standard investment calculations such as the internal rate of return, and for calculating loan variables such as the periodic payment. For example, to calculate the monthly payment on a $10,000 loan with 60 months, or periods, of payments and a 1% per month interest rate, you can use the loan payment function shown below:

=PMT(.01,60,1000)

About the interest rate argument

A common mistake when using financial functions is using an annual interest rate argument with a monthly periods argument. Note that in the preceding function example, a monthly loan payment is calculated. For this reason, the interest rate argument needs to be expressed as a monthly rate rather than as an annual rate.

 Arguments; Function Wizard

Finding Cells
Choose the Edit Find command to locate cells with specified contents: a fragment of text, part of a formula, a cell name or address, or a value.

Using the Edit Find Command

To use the Edit Find command, select the worksheet range Excel should search and then choose the command. If Excel finds a cell, it makes that cell active.

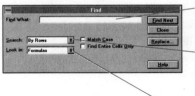

1 In the Find What text box, specify what you're looking for.

2 In the Search drop-down list box, indicate whether Excel should search column by column or row by row.

3 In the Look in drop-down list box, indicate where Excel should look: in formulas, at values, or in cell notes.

4 Find Next starts and restarts the search.

Considering Case in a Search

Use the Match Case and Find Entire Cells Only check boxes to indicate whether Excel should consider case (lower vs. upper) in its search and look for entire cells rather than a portion of a cell.

 Replacing Cell Contents

Finding Files You can use the File Find File command to locate workbooks based on characteristics of the file and summary information collected about the file. For step-by-step information on how to use this command to find a lost workbook, refer to **Troubleshooting: You Can't Find a Workbook**.

Fonts You can use a wide variety of fonts in your worksheets. With fonts, you can even include Greek symbols and other special characters. Here are a few examples:

Clean and attractive, Arial resembles Helvetica.

`Courier New looks like typewriter output.`

Times New Roman uses serifs—little cross-strokes—to make characters easier to read.

ΑΣΔΦαβχψυσΩΙΥ ————————— These are TrueType Symbol characters.

♋♑♒♌♏ ♓♋●♍♋♌♓ ———— These are TrueType WingDing characters.

🐾 **Changing Fonts**

Footers Page footers can be added to the bottom of printed worksheets and charts.

🐾 **Headers and Footers**

Formatting

You can add formatting to cells to control value punctuation, alignment of values and labels, font styles and point sizes, border lines, and background cell patterns. You can also add a special type of formatting, called **cell protection,** that prevents changes to cell contents and that hides cell formulas.

Adding background shading—**Patterns**
Adding border lines—**Borders**
Alignment of values and labels in cells—**Aligning Labels and Values**
Changing font styles and point sizes—**Fonts**
Formatting date values—**Date Formats**
Formatting time values—**Time Formats**
Preventing cell changes and hiding cell formulas—**Cell Protection**
Using (and reusing) formatting combinations—**Styles**
Value punctuation, including currency symbols and commas— **Formatting Numbers**

Formatting Numbers

You can add formatting to **values** in two ways: by including the formatting when you enter the value and by choosing the Format Cells command.

Formatting During Data Entry

Often the easier way is to include the formatting when you enter a value into the cell. This cell holds the value 12495.99. But because I entered $12,495.99 into the cell, Excel formats the cell so that the displayed value shows a dollar sign and a comma.

	A	B
1	$12,495.99	
2		

continues

Formatting Numbers *(continued)*

Formatting with the Format Cells Command

You can also format selected cells by choosing the Format Cells command and then selecting the Number tab.

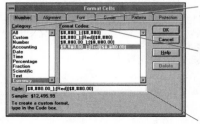

1 Select a formatting category from the Category list box.

2 Excel displays a list of the formatting choices in the Format Codes dialog box. You simply select one.

3 Look at the Sample field to see how the active cell looks with the selected format code.

Formula Bar   The formula bar is that space under the toolbars.

When you enter **labels**, **values**, and **formulas** into worksheet cells, Excel displays what you enter in the formula bar. If you select a cell by clicking, Excel also uses the formula bar to display the cell's contents. And if you click the formula, Excel lets you edit the cell's contents.

Formulas   In Excel, you use formulas to calculate **values.** To build a formula, select the cell where the formula should go, type the equals sign, =, to indicate that what you're about to type is a formula, and type the formula using standard arithmetic operators, values, **cell addresses,** and even cell names. If you use a cell address or a cell name, Excel uses the value stored in that cell. I know you did fine in third-grade arithmetic, but just to make sure you understand how all this works, here are some example formulas:

Formula	What happens
=2+2	Adds 2 and 2, returning the not-surprising result of 4
=24.5-12	Subtracts 12 from 24.5
=I81/U812	Divides the value in cell I81 by the value in cell U812
=RATE*PRINCIPAL	Multiplies the values in the cells named RATE and PRINCIPAL
=1000^2	Squares the value 1000

Excel applies the standard rules of operator precedence in a formula that uses more than one operator: Exponential operations are performed first, then division and multiplication, and then addition and subtraction. But you can override these standard rules by using parentheses. Excel will first perform operations inside parentheses. This probably makes perfect sense to some people, but just to beat this thing to death, here are some more example formulas. All use the same values and operators, but they return different results because of the way parentheses change the order of the arithmetic operations.

Formula	Result
=1+2*3	7
= (1+2)*3	9

⋰ Filtering Lists; Functions; Function Wizard; Subtotaling Lists

Selective formulas

If you want to count the times a particular value or label occurs in a range of cells or if you want to tally a value for some subset of the entries in a list (or if you want to do something that sounds like either of these tasks), choose the Data Filter and Data Subtotals commands. Together, they'll make these selective calculations easy and straightforward.

Fractions To enter a fraction in a cell, type the equals sign and then the fraction. In other words, enter a formula for the fraction. For example, to enter the fraction 1/4, type =1/4. Excel stores the equivalent decimal value for the fraction.

 Formulas

Full Screen You can use almost all of your screen to display a workbook's sheets. When you view a workbook in a full screen, Excel displays only the menu bar and the workbook. Excel doesn't display the toolbars, the application window's title bar, and the document window's title bar.

Viewing the Full Screen

To view the Excel application window as a full screen, choose the View Full Screen command.

Viewing the Regular Screen

To return to the regular view of the application window, choose the View Full Screen command again. Or click the Full Screen button.

Functions Functions are prefabricated **formulas** you can use to make worksheet construction easier—and more accurate. In a function, you name the formula to be calculated and supply the inputs, or **arguments.**

Conditional test or logical formulas—	**Conditional Functions**
Date and time value formulas—	**Date and Time Functions**
Depreciation, investment, and loan formulas—	**Financial Functions**

Logarithmic, mathematical, trigonometric formulas—**Math Functions**	
Statistics and database formulas—**Statistics Functions**	
Table lookup and reference functions formulas—**Lookup Functions**	
Text string formulas—**Text Functions**	
Workbook information formulas—**Workbook Functions**	

Function Wizard The Function Wizard enters functions into cells, and it also lets you use functions to quickly perform complicated calculations. In my humble opinion it's also the most useful new feature in Excel version 5.

To use the Function Wizard, follow these steps:

1 Choose the Insert Function command or the Function Wizard tool. Excel displays the first Function Wizard dialog box.

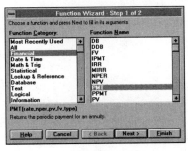

2 In the Function Category list box, select the general type of calculation you want. Excel displays a list of the functions in that category.

3 From the Function Name list, select the calculation you want.

4 Select Next to move to the second Function Wizard dialog box.

5 Using the text boxes, enter the function arguments as values, cell addresses, or cell names. Excel displays the function value to the right of the text box. (Required argument names appear in **bold**; optional argument names don't.)

6 To use another function's result as an argument, select the Function Wizard button just left of the argument's text box.

7 To place the function into the active cell, select Finish. (If you don't want to place the function into the active cell, select Cancel.)

⁂ Formulas

Goal Seek The Tools Goal Seek command calculates the formula
input value that causes the formula to return a specified
result. You use Goal Seek when you know what formula
result you want, but don't know what input value returns
the desired result. To illustrate how the Goal Seek command works, suppose you want to know what initial deposit, or present value, results in a future value formula of
$500,000 if the annual interest rate is 10% and the term is
25 years.

To use Goal Seek, follow these steps:

1 Build a worksheet that includes the future value formula and that
uses cell addresses as inputs. In the example you want to find the
initial deposit amount that causes the future value formula in cell
B4 to return $500,000.

	A	B	C
1	Initial Deposit	$10,000.00	
2	Annual Interest Rate	10%	
3	Years of Compounding	25	
4	Future Value	$108,347.06	
5			

2 Choose the Tools Goal Seek command.

3 Enter the cell address with the formula in the Set cell text box.

4 Enter the target value you want the formula to return in the To
value text box.

5 Enter the cell address with the input value that the Goal Seek
command should adjust in the By changing cell text box.

	A	B	C
1	Initial Deposit	$46,148.00	
2	Annual Interest Rate	10%	
3	Years of Compounding	25	
4	Future Value	$500,000.00	
5			

Once you've described the Goal Seek operation, Excel begins adjust-
ing the input value, looking for the value that causes the formula to
return the target value. If Goal Seek can find an input value that returns the desired target value, it displays a message box telling you so
and then adjusts the input value cell.

Go To You can move the cell selector to another location quickly using the Go To drop-down list box or the Edit Go To command.

Using the Go To Drop-down List Box

To quickly move the cell selector to a particular cell, activate the Go To drop-down list box.

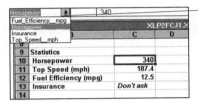

Type the cell address or select a cell name, and then press Enter.

Using the Go To Command

You can also use the Edit Go To command to quickly move to a cell.

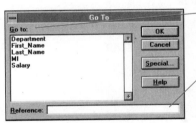

Excel lists any cell names you've defined in the Go To list box. Double-click on any of these to move the cell selector.

In the Reference text box, enter the address of the cell to which you want to move.

Select the Special button if you want to move the cell selector based on cell contents and characteristics. Excel displays the Select Special dialog box.

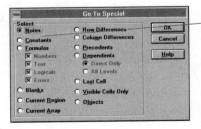

Use the Go To Special dialog box's radio buttons to indicate to what kind of cell the selector should be moved. Marking the Notes radio button, for example, tells Excel to move the cell selector to the first cell in the selected range with a note.

Gridlines

Gridlines are the intersecting horizontal and vertical lines that appear on both worksheets and charts.

Gridlines on charts—**Chart Gridlines**
Gridlines on printed worksheets—**Sheet Page Setup**
Worksheet gridlines appearance and color—**Worksheet Views**

Groups

A group is a range selection in two or more worksheets. You select a group by first making a range selection in the current worksheet and then selecting additional worksheets. Select additional worksheets by clicking the worksheet page tabs.

You can format groups using the Format Cells command. You can fill Groups too, using the Edit Fill Across Worksheets command.

❖ **Formatting**

Headers and Footers

Choose the File Page Setup command and select the Header/Footer tab to display a dialog box in which you'll specify how page headers and footers are formatted for printed worksheets and charts.

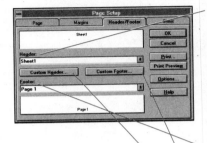

To add a standard header to printed pages, activate the Header drop-down list box and select a header style. Excel provides standard headers that name the sheet, number pages, and identify the author or user.

To add a standard footer to printed pages, activate the Footer drop-down list box and select a footer style.

Use the Custom Header and Customer Footer command buttons to tailor headers or footers to your own needs. Excel displays another dialog box you use to create a header or footer from scratch.

 Sheet Page Setup

Help

Need help with some Microsoft Excel task? No problem. Select the Help toolbar button. Excel adds a question mark to the mouse pointer arrow.

To indicate what you want help with, click on the menu command or on a part of a workbook or a window. After you select the item for which you want help, Excel starts the Help application, and Help displays specific information about your selection.

Hiding and Unhiding Sheets

You can hide the active sheet so that it isn't displayed in the workbook window. To do this, choose the Format Sheet Hide command.

To unhide hidden sheets in the selected worksheet group, choose the Format Sheet Unhide command.

🐾 **Groups**

Importing Spreadsheet Files

Excel lets you use files created with other spreadsheet programs. To use such a file, choose the File Open command. When Excel displays the Open dialog box, use the List Files of Type drop-down list box to specify which type of file you want to use.

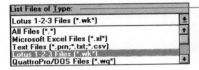

The List Files of Type drop-down list box identifies the file types you can easily import. All you do is open the file.

Importing Text Files; Opening Workbooks

Importing Text Files

Excel converts text files—for example, those created with a word processor—for use in an Excel workbook. To convert a text file, take the following steps:

1 Choose the File Open command to retrieve the file. Once you do this, Excel starts the Text Import Wizard.

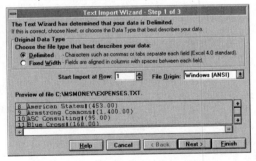

2 Mark the Delimited radio button if the fields, or chunks, of information are delimited. (Delimited means that the fields are separated with a character such as a Tab.)

3 Mark the Fixed Width radio button if the fields of information are arranged neatly into fixed-width columns. (A report that tabulates data would almost always be arranged this way, for example.)

4 Tell Excel which is the first line, or row, you want imported.

5 Specify the operating environment in which the file was created: Windows, Macintosh, MS-DOS, or OS/2. Excel displays the tentative organization of the converted text file at the bottom of the dialog box.

6 Select OK.

continues

Importing Text Files *(continued)*

7 If you are converting a delimited text file, you use the wizard's second dialog box to identify the delimiter—the character used to separate the chunks of information on a line.

8 Use the Data Preview area to verify the converted data.

9 If necessary, use the Treat consecutive delimiters as one check box and the Text Qualifier drop-down list box to adjust for any conversion problems. (A text qualifier is the character used by the delimited file to show the beginning and end of text labels.)

10 If you are converting a nondelimited file, click the mouse to show column borders. Excel adds a vertical arrow to show the border, or break, line.

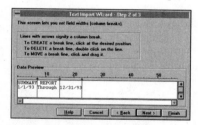

11 As necessary, remove border lines by double-clicking.

12 As necessary, move border lines by dragging.

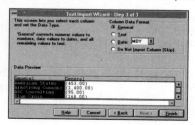

13 Select a column and then a format radio button.

14 Mark the Do Not Import Column (Skip) radio button if you don't want the text file field in the new Excel workbook.

15 Choose Finish to display the converted text file in an Excel workbook. (Once you get the converted text file in an Excel workbook, you'll want to adjust column widths. Be sure also to save the new workbook with the converted text file data.)

 Columns; Saving Workbooks

For your information

All database and most accounting applications create delimited text files for easy importing into programs such as Microsoft Excel.

Inserting
You can add, or insert, cells, charts, columns, functions, macros, names, notes, page breaks, pictures, objects, rows, and worksheets.

Adding cell notes—**Notes**	
Adding cells—**Inserting Cells**	
Adding charts—**ChartWizard**	
Adding columns—**Inserting Columns**	
Adding functions—**Function Wizard**	
Adding macros—**Macro**	
Adding names—**Names**	
Adding objects—**Object Linking and Embedding**	
Adding page breaks—**Page Breaks**	
Adding pictures—**Worksheet Pictures**	
Adding rows—**Inserting Rows**	
Adding worksheets—**Inserting Worksheets**	

Formula adjustments
Excel adjusts formulas when you insert cells, columns, rows, and worksheets.

Inserting Cells
You can insert single cells or groups of cells into rows and columns.

Inserting a Single Cell
Select the cell that occupies the position you want for the new, inserted cell and then choose the Insert Cells command and complete the Insert dialog box.

Use the Insert radio buttons to indicate how Excel should make room for the new cell or cells: by moving down the cells in the selected column (indicated as Shift Cells Down) or by moving right the cells in the selected row (indicated as Shift Cells Right).

Don't use the Entire Row or Entire Column radio buttons unless you want to insert a new row above the active cell or a new column left of the active cell.

Inserting Several Cells
Select a range of cells so that the top- or left-selected cell occupies the position you want for the top or left new, inserted cell; then choose the Insert Cells command and complete the Insert dialog box. (Excel inserts as many cells as you select.)

∴ **Inserting Columns; Inserting Rows**

Inserting Columns
You can insert single columns or groups of columns into a worksheet.

Inserting a Single Column
Select the column that occupies the position you want for the new, inserted column; then choose the Insert Columns command.

Inserting Several Columns

Select a range of columns so that the leftmost selected column occupies the position you want for the leftmost inserted column; then choose the Insert Columns command. (Excel inserts as many columns as you select.)

❖ **Inserting Cells**

Inserting Rows
Just as you can insert one or more columns in a worksheet, you can also insert one or more rows.

Inserting a Single Row

Select the row that occupies the position you want for the new, inserted row; then choose the Insert Rows command.

Inserting Several Rows

Select a range of rows so that the topmost selected row occupies the position you want for the topmost inserted column; then choose the Insert Rows command. Excel inserts as many rows as you select.

❖ **Inserting Cells; Inserting Columns**

Inserting Worksheets
You can insert as many worksheets as you like in workbooks.

Inserting a Single Worksheet

Select the sheet that occupies the position you want for the new, inserted worksheet; then choose the Insert Worksheets command.

Inserting Several Worksheets

Select a range of worksheets so that the first selected worksheet occupies the position you want for the first inserted worksheet; then choose the Insert Worksheets command. (Excel inserts as many worksheets as you select.)

❖ **Inserting Cells**

Italic Characters

You can *italicize* characters in the current worksheet selection by pressing Ctrl+I or by clicking the Italic Formatting toolbar button. You can also use the Format Cells command and its Font tab options.

> *:* **Changing Fonts**

Labels

A label is something you enter into a cell but that you don't want to later use in a formula. Usually, a label is a chunk of text or a chunk of text and numbers. But a label might use numbers and still not be something you later want to use in a formula. For example, a telephone number uses numbers, but you probably wouldn't ever use a telephone number in a formula.

> *:* **Entering Data; Values**

List Management

Excel provides a simple database management feature called List Management. You can sort lists, filter them, and subtotal list entries. And you can create PivotTables based on lists.

Analyzing lists—**Pivot Tables**
Arranging and organizing lists—**Sorting Lists**
Building lists—**Creating Lists**
Creating a new list using a list—**Filtering Lists**
Editing entries in a list—**Editing Lists**
Finding a list entry—**Searching Lists**
Removing, or deleting, entries from a list—**Editing Lists**

Lookup Functions

Lookup functions return specified values or labels from tables or arrays. For example, the following function returns the second label—which is CA—in the array of labels included as arguments:

Lookup formulas specify which value or label should be returned using one argument.

=CHOOSE(2,"AZ","CA","ID","MT")

Lookup formulas also specify where the function should look for the specified value.

⁝⁝ Argument; Function Wizard

Lotus 1-2-3 Lotus 1-2-3 is another spreadsheet program—as you undoubtedly know. What you may not know is that you can open and save Lotus 1-2-3 worksheet files with Microsoft Excel. To do this, you use the Open and Save dialog boxes' List Files of Type list box to specify a Lotus 1-2-3 file format.

⁝⁝ Opening Workbooks; Saving Workbooks

Lotus Improv Lotus Improv is also a spreadsheet program—as you may not know. Because Lotus Improv uses an unusual worksheet structure, it's not very easy to move Improv worksheets, which are called models, to other spreadsheet programs such as Excel. If you want to try, save and open worksheets in the Lotus 1-2-3 file format.

⁝⁝ Opening Workbooks; Saving Workbooks

Intrigued by Lotus Improv?

You can use Excel's PivotTable command to organize and reorganize worksheet data in many of the same ways as you can in Lotus Improv.

Macro A macro is simply a series of commands. This doesn't sound very exciting, of course. And maybe it isn't. But you can store macros in separate workbook sheets called, cleverly enough, macro sheets. And you can repeat them, or play them back. With this play-back ability, you can use macros to automate operations that work the same way every time you use them.

 Visual Basic

Margins Choose the File Page Setup command and select the Margin tab to display a dialog box in which you can specify page margins for printed worksheets and charts.

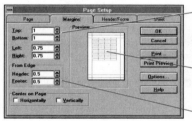

Use the Top, Bottom, Left, and Right boxes to specify the margin in inches.

Look at the Preview box to see the effect of your specifications.

Use the Header and Footer boxes to specify how many inches a header and footer should be from the edge of the page.

 Printing

Math Functions Excel's rich set of arithmetic, logarithmic, and trigonometric functions make for quick mathematical **formulas.** Here's a sampling of what they can do:

Function	What it does
=COS(.5)	Returns the cosine of 0.5, which is 0.877582562
=LOG10(100)	Returns the common logarithm of 100, which is 2
=SQRT(9)	Returns the square root of 9, which is 3

 **Argument; Function Wizard**

Microsoft Word You can use Microsoft Excel worksheets and charts in your Word documents.

Using Excel Worksheets and Charts with Word

Select the worksheet range or chart and choose the Edit Copy command. Switch to the Word application, position the insertion point where you want the worksheet or chart, and choose the Edit Paste command.

⋮ Object Linking and Embedding; Switching Tasks

Moving and Copying Sheets You can reshuffle the sheets in a workbook by moving (and copying) them. To move a sheet, follow these steps:

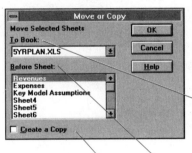

1 Activate the sheet, for example, by clicking on its tab.

2 Choose the Edit Move/Copy Sheet command.

3 Use the To Book drop-down list box to name the workbook to which you want to copy or move the sheet. (The workbook must be open.)

4 Use the Before Sheet list box to indicate in front of which sheet you want to copy or move the sheet.

5 Mark the Create a Copy check box to copy, or duplicate, the sheet rather than move it.

⋮ Chart Sheets; Worksheets

Moving Data

You can move data—**values, labels, formulas,** and worksheet ranges—with either the mouse or the Edit Cut and Edit Paste commands.

Moving Data with the Mouse

To move data with the mouse, select what you want to move, then click on the selection border, and then drag the selection.

Moving Data with Edit Cut and Edit Paste

To move data with the Edit Cut and Edit Paste commands, follow these steps:

1 Select the cell or worksheet range you want to move.

2 Choose Edit Cut.

3 Select the cell to which the copied cell should be moved, or select the cell to which the upper left corner cell of the worksheet range should be moved.

4 Choose Edit Paste.

∴ **Copying Data**

Moving formulas

When you move a formula, Excel doesn't adjust relative cell references in it.

Moving Objects and Pictures

You can move drawing objects and pictures with the mouse or with commands.

Moving with the Mouse

Simply select the object or picture and then drag it to where you want it.

Excel adds selection handles to the object or picture to show you've selected it. The selection handles are the little black squares appearing at the corners and along each edge.

Moving with Commands

You can also move a graphic object or picture using the Edit Cut and Edit Paste commands in the same way you move other types of worksheet data.

:· **Copying Objects and Pictures; Resizing Pictures; Worksheet Pictures**

Names You can name a cell or a range of cells and then refer to that name in **formulas** and in command **dialog boxes.** To name a cell, follow these steps:

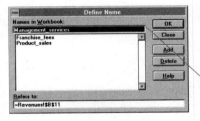

1 Select the cell or range of cells.

2 Choose the Insert Name Define command. Excel displays the Define Name dialog box.

3 Enter the cell or range name into the Names in Workbook text box.

4 Excel lists any cell names already given.

Naming Sheets Excel provides default names for **worksheets** and **chart sheets**—Sheet1, Sheet2, Chart1, and so on—but these names aren't very descriptive.

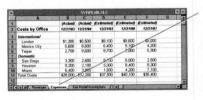

You can use sheet names to organize your workbooks. To replace Excel's default names, double-click the sheet tab or choose the Format Sheet Rename command.

In the Rename Sheet dialog box, replace the existing sheet name by typing over it in the Name text box.

New Workbooks
To create a new workbook, choose the File New command. Not very difficult, eh?

⁂ Opening Workbooks; Workbooks

Notes
You can use cell notes to document or describe the contents of a cell.

Adding and Editing Notes
To enter or edit a cell note, follow these steps:

1 Select the cell.

2 Choose the Insert Note command.

3 In the Text Note area, type your note.

4 Get really wacky, and you can add sounds to the cell using the Sound Note command buttons. (To do this, use the Import command to tell Excel which WAV audio file holds the sound note.)

Locating Notes
To see a cell note, select the cell and choose the Insert Note command.

Domestic	
San Diego	3,300
Houston	9,200
Miami	6,400

To show you which cells have notes, Excel places a marker in the cell's upper right corner.

Object Linking and Embedding Object linking and embedding, or OLE (oh-lay), is a Windows feature.

What OLE Does

You use OLE to create what's called a compound document—a document file that combines two or more types of documents. For example, you might want to create a compound document that includes a long report written in, for example, Word for Windows or WordPerfect. On page 27 of your report, however, you might want to include a worksheet (or worksheet fragment) created in Excel. And perhaps on page 37 of your report, you might want to include a chart created in Excel. So your compound document really consists of stuff created in different applications and pasted together into one big, compound document.

Using OLE to Create Compound Documents

To do all this pasting together and combining, you can often use the application's Edit Copy and Edit Paste (or Edit Paste Special) commands. And if you're creating the compound document in Excel, you can use the Insert Object command.

Distinguishing Between Linked Objects and Embedded Objects

A linked object—remember this might be the Excel worksheet you've pasted into a word-processing document—gets updated whenever the source document changes. An embedded object doesn't. (You can, however, double-click on an embedded object to open the application that created the embedded object to make your changes.)

> **Embedding and Linking Existing Objects; Embedding New Objects**

What you absolutely need to know about OLE

Perhaps the most important tidbit for you to know about OLE is that it's very easy to use. You don't have to do anything other than copy and paste the things—called objects—you want to plop into the compound document.

Opening Workbooks
To open a previously saved workbook, choose the File Open command.

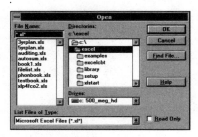

1 Use the Directories and Drives list boxes to specify where the workbook file was saved.

2 Use the List Files of Type list box if you want to open a file with a format other than that of the usual Excel workbook file. (You might do this if you want to import another spreadsheet program's file.)

3 Use the File Name text box or the File Name list box to identify the file.

Default Workbooks; File Summary; Saving Workbooks; Troubleshooting: You Can't Find a Workbook

Protecting the original workbook

If you don't want to overwrite the original workbook file, mark the Read Only check box. If you mark this check box and later want to save the workbook, you'll need to use a new file name.

Page Breaks

Excel breaks worksheets into page-sized chunks automatically as it prints. You can let Excel determine these page breaks, or you can choose where these page breaks occur.

Adding Vertical Page Breaks

Select the column just right of where the worksheet should be vertically split into separate pages, and then choose the Insert Page Break command.

Adding Horizontal Page Breaks

Select the row just below where the worksheet should be horizontally split into separate pages, and then choose the Insert Page Break command.

Removing Page Breaks

Select the column just right of or the row just below the page break, and then choose the Insert Remove Page Break command.

Excel draws a dashed line wherever page breaks occur.

 Printing

Page Numbers

You add page numbers to printed worksheets and charts by adding a header or a footer that includes a page number. You can specify which number Excel uses for the first page. For example, the first page of a printed worksheet shouldn't be numbered 1 if it's the 26th page in a report; it should be numbered 26.

Headers and Footers; Printed Pages Setup

Page Setup Choose the File Page Setup command and its tab
options—Page, Margins, Header/Footer, Sheet, and
Chart—to control the appearance of printed worksheets
and charts.

Chart appearance—**Chart Page Setup**	
Page appearance—**Printed Pages Setup**	
Page headers and page footers———**Headers and Footers**	
Page margins—**Margins**	
Sheet appearance—**Sheet Page Setup**	

Page Tab Excel uses page tabs in several ways. One use is to label
the workbook sheet. (You can also click sheet page tabs to
move through a workbook.) Another use of page tabs appears in some dialog boxes. If a dialog box shows more
than will fit within its border, the dialog box uses several
pages. Each page then collects a related set of needed input information.

You can move through these pages by clicking on the
page tabs. To see an example of how this works, choose
the File Page Setup command and then click on the page
tabs—Page, Margins, Header/Footer, and Sheet. I'm not
going to include a figure that shows this. I don't want to
ruin the surprise for you.

❖ **Naming Sheets**

Pagination Pagination refers to the process of breaking a document into page-sized chunks. You can let Excel paginate
your documents. You do this simply by printing the
workbook or by print previewing the workbook. Or you
can do it yourself using hard page breaks. You do this
with the Insert Page Breaks command.

❖ **Page Breaks; Printing; Print Preview**

Passwords You can use passwords to limit access to workbooks, to limit changes to workbook files, and to limit changes to cell contents.

Controlling access to workbook files—**Save Options**

Protecting cells in a workbook—**Cell Protection**

Patterns To add background patterns to cells, choose the Format Cells command and the Patterns tab.

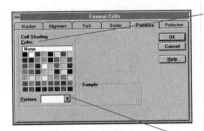

Select the foreground color for the pattern using the colored Cell Shading buttons.

Activate the Pattern list box to choose a pattern and the color for the lines, dots, or cross-hatching that create the pattern.

Percentages Percentages are decimal values such as 0.75 formatted as 75%. To store percentages in cells, you can enter them as decimal values and then format them, or you can enter them as percentages. (In this case, Excel stores the decimal value in the cell but formats the decimal value as a percentage.)

.·. **Entering Data; Formatting Numbers**

Picture Charts

A picture chart uses little pictures in place of the standard chart **data markers** such as pie slices, bars, or lines. You can replace the standard data markers Excel uses for charts—columns, lines, and pie slices—with clip art images. To create a picture chart, follow these steps:

1 Plot your data in a bar, column, or line chart.

2 Copy the picture you want to use in place of the standard data marker to the clipboard. (You can do this by inserting a picture in an Excel workbook, selecting the picture, and then choosing Edit Copy.)

3 Display the chart.

4 Select the data markers you want to replace—for example, by clicking.

5 Choose Edit Paste.

  Clip Art; Clipboard; Worksheet Pictures

PivotTables

PivotTables organize list entries in ways that make the information easier to analyze and understand.

	A	B	C
1	State	Customer	Revenue
2	WA	DeLaurenti Food Corp	$14,700.00
3	WA	Edwards Realty	28,300.00
4	WA	Foles Dry Cleaning	9,200.00
5	CA	Gonzalez & Shearson, Attorneys	36,200.00
6	CA	Hapsburg Restaurant	14,700.00
7	CA	Ito & Company	6,100.00
8	OR	Johnson Motors	18,700.00
9	CA	Kirkland Landscaping	46,900.00
10	CA	Land Management, Inc.	39,000.00
11	MT	Party-Time Supply Company	41,400.00
12	MT	Belcher Construction	4,700.00
13	ID	Sunseri Corporation	900.00
14	ID	Junebug's Antiques	5,500.00
15	ID	Rover's Dog Food	20,000.00

You create PivotTables for lists such as this. The PivotTable in this example could give the number of customers in each state and the sum of revenue for those customers.

To create a PivotTable for a list, follow these steps:

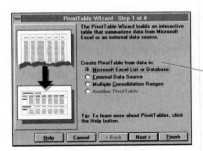

1 Select the list (including headers).

2 Choose the Data PivotTable command. Excel starts the PivotTable Wizard.

3 Indicate the source you'll use for creating the PivotTable and then select Next. Usually, you'll use a list, so you mark the first radio button. You can use an external data source, another PivotTable, or a consolidated range

4 Confirm the data source and then select Next. If you use a list, for example, the second PivotTable Wizard dialog box asks for the worksheet range holding the list. (The appearance of the second PivotTable Wizard dialog box depends on the data source used for the PivotTable.)

5 Optionally, select Browse to display a dialog box you can use to open another workbook file—if that's where the list is.

continues

99

PivotTables *(continued)*

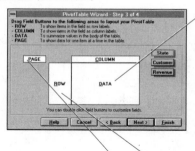

6 Drag the button for the list field you want to summarize to the DATA block. By default, the PivotTable Wizard assumes you want to sum values and count labels. But double-click the button to display a dialog box you can use to select another summary calculation.

7 Drag the button for the list field that should show in rows to the ROW block.

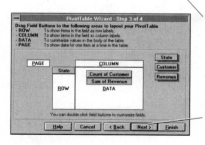

8 To arrange list information onto separate worksheet pages or into separate columns, drag buttons to the PAGE or COLUMN blocks.

9 Select Next when you've described how the PivotTable should look.

10 Use the PivotTable Starting Cell text box to give the upper left corner of the worksheet range where you want the PivotTable placed— such as A1 of a new worksheet.

11 Use the PivotTable Name text box to name or describe the Pivot-Table. A Pivot-Table that summarizes client revenue by state, for example, might be named "Clients by State."

12 Use PivotTable Options check boxes to indicate where grand totals should be calculated, whether the PivotTable data should be saved, and whether Excel should Auto-Format the table.

13 Select Finish. Excel creates a PivotTable that summarizes the list information in a table.

	A	B	C
1	State	Data	Total
2	CA	Count of Customer	5
3		Sum of Revenue	142900
4	ID	Count of Customer	3
5		Sum of Revenue	26400
6	MT	Count of Customer	2
7		Sum of Revenue	46100
8	OR	Count of Customer	1
9		Sum of Revenue	18700
10	WA	Count of Customer	3
11		Sum of Revenue	52200
12	Total Count of Customer		14
13	Total Sum of Revenue		286300

Changing PivotTable Organization

You can change the organization of a PivotTable by dragging the list field buttons; drag the State button to the Data button, for example, and Excel flip-flops the PivotTable.

	A	B	C
1	Data	State	Total
2	Count of Customer	CA	5
3		ID	3
4		MT	2
5		OR	1
6		WA	3
7	Sum of Revenue	CA	142900
8		ID	26400
9		MT	46100
10		OR	18700
11		WA	52200
12	Total Count of Customer		14
13	Total Sum of Revenue		286300

Creating Lists

Points One point equals 1/72 inch. In Excel, you specify font size and row height in points.

🐾 **Fonts; Rows**

Of row heights and font sizes

Funny thing, but a 12-point font won't fit in a row measuring 12 points in height. For this reason, your row height point size setting needs to exceed your font point size setting.

Precedents Precedents are cells that supply other cells' formulas with values. For example, if the formula in cell A1 references cells B12 and E6, the values in cells B12 or E6 must be supplied before the formula in A1 calculates. Cells B12 and E6, then, are precedent cells for A1.

🐾 **Auditing Worksheets; Dependents**

Printed Pages Setup Choose the File Page Setup command and select the Page tab to display a dialog box you'll use to specify how pages should print.

1 Use the Orientation radio buttons to specify whether pages should be printed portrait or landscape.

2 Use the Scaling radio button and box to change the size of the printed worksheet or chart by a set percentage.

3 Use the Paper Size and Print Quality drop-down list boxes to choose a different paper size (assuming your printer supports this) and to change the print quality.

4 Tell Excel the page number to assign to the first printed page using the First Page Number text box.

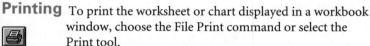

Printing To print the worksheet or chart displayed in a workbook window, choose the File Print command or select the Print tool.

If you choose the File Print command, Excel displays the Print dialog box. Use it to control how Excel prints the worksheet or chart.

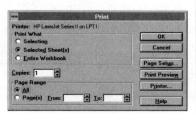

1 Use the Print What radio buttons to indicate whether you want to print the Selection (just the currently selected worksheet range), the Selected Sheets (the sheet that shows plus any others you've selected by pressing Ctrl or Shift and clicking), or the Entire Workbook (all the worksheets and charts in the workbook).

2 Use the Range radio buttons and boxes to indicate whether Excel should print all the pages you've indicated by your Print setting (the usual case) or only a range of pages indicated by your Print setting.

3 Select OK to print the worksheet.

 **Print Preview**

Print Preview Choose the File Print Preview command or select the Print Preview tool when you want to see how a workbook's pages will look before you print them. When you choose the command, Excel displays the Print Preview window.

continues

Print Preview *(continued)*

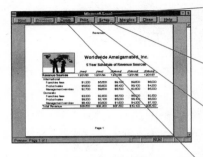

Use the Next and Previous buttons to page back and forth through the printed workbook pages.

Select the Setup button to display the Page Setup dialog box.

Select the Print button to print the workbook. But you probably figured this out yourself, right?

Use the Zoom command button to enlarge or reduce the printed page size.

Select the Margins button to tell Excel to display margin lines on the Print Preview window's pages.

You can change the page margins by dragging these margin lines.

❖ **Printed Pages Setup; Printing**

Quattro Pro Quattro Pro is a spreadsheet program. You can move worksheets between Quattro Pro and Microsoft Excel. Simply specify a Lotus 1-2-3 file format when you save and open the worksheets you want to move.

❖ **Opening Workbooks; Saving Workbooks**

Range Address A range address identifies the cells included in a rectangular chunk of a worksheet. A range address consists of the upper left and lower right corner cell addresses, separated by a colon.

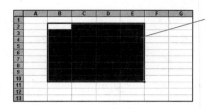

The selected range's address is B2:E10.

Lotus 1-2-3 and range addresses

If you've looked up this entry because you're a Lotus 1-2-3 user and you're having trouble specifying range addresses in Excel, let me make an observation. Your problem—if you want to call it that— probably isn't that you can't figure out how to type some range address such as B2:E10. Your problem is that in Excel you need to select the range before you choose commands rather than after you choose them. For example, in Excel to erase the contents of the range B2:E10, you select the range and then choose the Edit Clear command. In comparison, in Lotus 1-2-3, you would first choose the command Range Erase and then specify the range B2..E10. I hope that helps.

Relative Cell Address A relative cell address is a **cell address** that, if it's part of a copied formula, Excel adjusts. OK. That sounds complicated, but here's an example.

	A	B
1	10000	
2	10500	
3	11025	
4		

Say that cell A2 holds the formula =A1*1.05. Excel assumes the cell address in the formula, A1, is relative to the formula location in cell A2.

If you copy the formula from cell A2 to cell A3, Excel adjusts the formula to read =A2*1.05. Be- cause you've moved the formula down one row, Excel moves all the for- mula cell addresses down one row too.

⁘ **Absolute Cell Address; Copying Formulas; Formulas**

Removing Styles To remove, or delete, a style, or a combination of formatting choices, follow these steps:

1 Choose the Format Style command. Excel, instantly knowing what you're up to, displays the Style dialog box.

2 Select the style from the Style Name combo box.

3 Select the Delete command button.

 Adding Styles

Repeat You can usually repeat your last change to a workbook by choosing the Edit Repeat command or by selecting the Repeat tool.

 Undo

Replacing Cell Contents Choose the Edit Replace command to locate cells with specified contents—a fragment of text, part of a formula, a cell name, cell address, or value—and then replace these contents. To use the Edit Replace command, follow these steps:

1 Select the worksheet range Excel should search.

2 Choose the Edit Replace command.

3 In the Find What text box, specify what you want to replace.

4 In the Replace with text box, specify the replacement text.

5 In the Search drop-down list box, indicate whether Excel should search column by column or row by row.

6 In the Match Case and Find Whole Words Only check boxes, indicate whether Excel should consider case (lower vs. upper) in its search and look for whole words rather than partial words.

7 Select Find Next to start and restart the search.

8 Select Replace to substitute the replacement text in the active cell.

9 Select Replace All to substitute the replacement text in all cells in the selected area.

 Finding Cells

Reports A report describes the worksheet or worksheet ranges you want to print. If you've created views and scenarios, you can also include different views or scenarios in a report.

Creating a Report

Choose the File Print Report command. Then select the Add command button so that Excel displays the Add Report dialog box. You use it to describe the report.

Indicate which sheets should be included in the report.

Indicate which views and scenarios should be included in the report if your workbook includes these views and scenarios.

continues

Reports (continued)

Printing a Report

Choose the File Print Report command. Then select the report from the Reports list box and select OK. Excel prints your report.

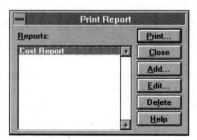

Resizing Pictures Use the mouse to resize drawing objects and pictures. To do this, select the object or picture. Excel marks the object or picture with selection handles. (The selection handles, as you may already know, are those little black squares.) To change the object's or picture's size, drag the selection handles.

   ❖ **Copying Objects and Pictures; Moving Objects and Pictures; Worksheet Pictures**

Rows You can change the height of rows with the mouse or with the Format Row submenu commands, but using the mouse is usually easier. To change the height of a selected row or of several selected rows with the mouse, drag the edge of the row label floor up or down.

Drag the edge of the row label floor up or down to change a row's height. Excel changes the mouse pointer to a two-directional arrow when you position the mouse pointer on the row floor.

   ❖ **Columns**

Save Options

The File Save As dialog box provides a command button, Options, which lets you protect workbook files from accidental deletion and from people who don't have a password to view the workbook.

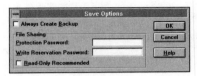

1 Mark the Always Create Backup check box to create a backup copy of the existing, or old, workbook file whenever you save a new copy of the workbook file.

2 You can limit viewing of the file by assigning a protection password. Excel asks for the protection password when someone attempts to open the workbook file using the File Open command.

3 Limit changes to the file by assigning a write reservation password. Excel asks for the write reservation password when someone attempts to save the workbook file using the File Save command. (Even with a write reservation password, someone can still save a copy of the workbook file with a new name.)

4 Mark the Read-Only Recommended check box if you want Excel to display a message that suggests someone open the file with read-only privileges. By opening the workbook file as read-only, you can't later save it except by giving it a new name.

:: File Summary; Passwords; Saving Workbooks

Saving Workbooks

To save workbooks and the worksheets and charts they contain, you use either the File Save or the File Save As command.

Resaving a Workbook

Choose the File Save command when you have saved the workbook before and want to save the workbook using the same name and in the same location.

continues

Saving Workbooks (continued)

Saving a Workbook for the First Time

Choose the File Save As command when you haven't yet saved the workbook or you want to save it with a new name or in a new location.

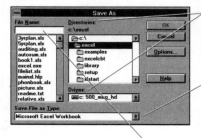

1 In the Directories and Drives list boxes, specify where the workbook file should be placed.

2 Use the Save File As Type list box to save the file in a format other the usual Excel workbook file format. (Do this, for example, to use the workbook file with another spreadsheet program.)

3 In the File Name text box, name the workbook file, but don't enter the file extension. Excel adds this for you because it uses the file extension to identify the file type.

⁝⁝ File Summary; Opening Workbooks; Save Options

Scenarios When you boil it down, a scenario is a collection of values or inputs for specified cells. All you do is store a set of inputs and give the set a name using the Tools Scenario Manager command. When you want to reuse the inputs, you choose the Tools Scenario Manager command to indicate which set of inputs you want to use. In effect, then, you get to change as many inputs at once using a command rather than having to individually change values in cells.

Scientific Notation

If a cell uses the general number format, Excel uses scientific notation to display values that are too big or too small to fit neatly within the cell's width.

	A	B
1	3E+08	
2	1E-07	
3		

The value 300,000,000 is too big to fit neatly into the standard width cell, so Excel displays this value as 3E+08, which is equivalent to 3×10^8.

The value 0.0000001 is too small to fit neatly into the standard width cell, so Excel displays this value as 1E-07, which is equivalent to 1×10^{-7}.

If a value is very large or very small, Excel may even store a value in the cell that uses scientific notation. For example, you type the digit 3 followed by 21 zeroes:

3000000000000000000000

This value is large in the truest sense, right? Excel agrees. So it uses the scientific notation, 3E+21, both for storing and for displaying the value.

Entering Data; Formatting Numbers

Entering values with scientific notation

You can use scientific notation to enter values into cells too. Although Excel uses an uppercase letter E for scientific notation, you can type either an uppercase E or a lowercase e.

Scrolling

Scrolling simply refers to paging up and down and left and right in a **workbook**. You can use the horizontal and vertical scroll bars to scroll up and down and right and left if you've got a mouse.

continues

Scrolling *(continued)*

You can also scroll with the keyboard. You can use the PageUp and PageDown keys to scroll up and down. And you can use the Tab and Shift+Tab keys to scroll right and left.

Go To; Window Panes

Creating nonscrollable columns and rows

If you use columns and rows to label your worksheet contents, you may not want these labeling columns and rows to scroll. You may want them fixed, or unscrollable. You can do this by by creating **window panes**.

Searching Lists To search a list, follow these steps:

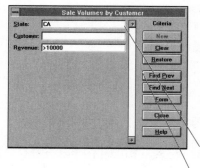

1 Select the list (including the headers).

2 Choose the Data Form command.

3 Select the Criteria command button. Excel displays the criteria entry version of the Data Form dialog box.

4 Use the text boxes to describe the list entry you want to find.

5 Use the Find Prev and Find Next command buttons to search backward and forward in a list.

If you enter stuff into the text boxes, Excel looks for an entry that exactly matches what you enter.

You can also search for values based on a conditional, or **Boolean algebra,** test. Here, for example, the criterion >10000 says find clients providing more than $10,000 of revenue.

All the criteria you enter are used in the search. By entering both a State and a Revenue criterion, as shown here, Excel looks only for California clients providing $10,000 of revenue or more. Note that you don't have to enter the header, or field, name.

When Excel finds a list entry matching your criteria, it displays the list entry in the Data Form dialog box. To continue looking through the list, use the Find Prev and Find Next command buttons. To return to the criteria entry version of the Data Form dialog box—perhaps to specify some new criteria—select the Criteria command button.

Creating Lists

Selecting Cells
You select single cells by clicking and dragging or using the direction keys. (The cell you select is called the **active cell**.)

Selecting a Single Cell
Click on the cell or use the direction keys to move the cell selector to the cell.

Selecting Rectangular Ranges of Cells
You can select more than one cell—what's called a range—by dragging the mouse between opposite corners of the range. Or you can select a cell, hold down Shift, and then use the direction keys to select a rectangle of cells. (In a rectangle, or range, selection, one cell will still be the active cell.)

Selecting Multiple Ranges of Cells
You can also select discontinuous rectangles of cells by holding down Ctrl and then dragging the mouse between the opposite corners of each range.

Selecting Columns You select a column by clicking on the
column letter label. You select a range of columns by
clicking on the first column and dragging the mouse to
the last column.

Selecting Rows You select a single row by clicking on the row
number label. You select a range of rows by clicking on
the first row and dragging the mouse to the last row.

Sharing Microsoft Excel Data You can easily share
values, labels, formulas, worksheet ranges, and **charts**
created in Excel with other Windows applications. To
share, follow these steps:

1 Select what you want to share: a worksheet range, a chart, some
formula fragment, or anything else.

2 Choose the Edit Copy command.

3 Switch to the other application using the Control-menu's Switch
To command.

4 Display the document in which you want to place the Excel information.

5 Paste the contents of the Clipboard into the other application's
document. (Probably, you'll do so with that application's Edit Paste
command.)

⁖ **Clipboard; Object Linking and Embedding; Switching
Tasks**

To link or to embed—that is the question

When Windows pastes an object—a worksheet fragment, for example—into another application's document, you'll usually have a choice as to whether the
pasted object is linked to the source document or is merely an embedded copy of
the source document. Use the Paste Special command to make your choice.

Sheet Page Setup Choose the File Page Setup command and mark the Sheet tab to display a dialog box you'll use to specify how worksheets should appear on printed pages. (The active sheet must display a worksheet for this tab to appear.)

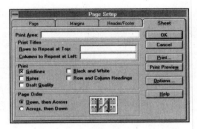

1 Use the Print Area text box to limit the printed portion of the worksheet to a range such as A1:G3. To specify multiple ranges, place commas between the individual ranges, for example, A1:G30, A35:G75.

2 Use the Print Titles text boxes to indicate whether each printed worksheet page should show a column or a row or a set of columns or rows. Do this if you've used rows or columns to hold headings that you want appear on each page.

3 Use the Print check boxes to indicate whether worksheet gridlines, cell notes, and row numbers and column letters, for example, should print.

4 Use the Page Order radio buttons to indicate the order in which Excel should print the page-sized chunks of a worksheet that takes more than a single page to print.

Sheets Sheets are the pages of a workbook that Excel uses to show **worksheets, chart sheets,** and, in rare circumstances, macro sheets.

Shortcut Menus Excel knows which commands make sense in which situations. It also knows which commands you, as an Excel user, are most likely to use. If you want, Excel will display a menu of these commands—called the Shortcut menu. All you need to do is click the right button on the mouse.

Solver The Tools Solver command lets you solve optimization modeling problems. In an optimization modeling problem, you maximize or minimize an objective function but subject it to constraints. The Solver isn't difficult to use—as long as you understand how optimization modeling techniques work.

Sorting Lists If you've defined a list using the Data Form command, you can sort the entries alphabetically based on a field that stores labels or in ascending or descending order based on a field that stores a value. To sort a list, follow these steps:

1 Select the list entries.

2 Choose the Data Sort command.

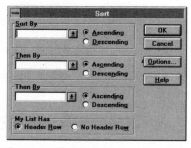

3 Use the Sort By drop-down list box to name the field used for alphabetizing or ordering.

4 Use the Sort By radio buttons to indicate whether you want alphabetic list entries arranged in A to Z or Z to A order or whether you want value list entries arranged in ascending or descending order.

5 Use the Then By drop-down list boxes and radio button sets to add second and third sorting keys.

6 Use the My List Has radio buttons to indicate whether the first selected row names the fields.

⁛ Creating Lists

The Sort tool

You can use the Sort tool to arrange the selected list entries in either ascending or descending order based on the first field.

Spelling You can use the Tools Spelling command to check the spelling of words used in labels. To use the command, select the worksheet area you want to spell-check (if you're interested in checking only a limited area). Excel displays the Spelling dialog box. Use it to control how Excel spell-checks and what Excel does when it finds a possible error.

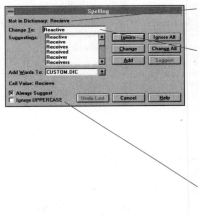

1 Excel alerts you to words it can't find in its dictionary.

2 Excel suggests an alternative spelling with the Change To text box if the Always Suggest check box is marked. You can edit whatever Excel suggests or select another word from the Suggestions list box

3 Indicate whether case should be considered in the spell-checking.

Using the Spelling Command Buttons

Once Excel finds a potentially misspelled word, you use the Spelling command buttons to indicate what Excel should do:

Button	What it does
Ignore	Ignore only this occurrence of the word.
Ignore All	Ignore this and every other occurrence of the word.
Change	Change this occurrence of the word to what the Change To text box shows.
Change All	Change this and every other occurrence of the word to what the Change To text box shows.
Add	Add the word to the spelling dictionary named in the Add Words To combo box.
Suggest	Look through the Excel spelling dictionary and the custom dictionary named in the Add Words To combo box for similarly spelled words.

continues

117

Spelling *(continued)*

If Excel can't find your word

You can use the wildcard characters ? and * in the Change To text box to find words spelled similarly to what you enter. You can use the * character to represent any combination of characters, and you can use the ? character to represent any single character. For example, if you're trying to spell the word that starts with the letters "Colo" but you don't know which letters follow—and Excel doesn't either—type Colo* in the Change To text box; then select Suggest. Excel will find all the words in its dictionary that start with letters "Colo."

Starting Excel
You start Excel the same way you start any Windows application.

Starting Excel Manually

To start Excel manually, follow these steps:

1 Start Windows—for example, by typing *win* at the MS-DOS prompt.

2 Display the program group in which Excel is an item. For example, if Excel's program group is Microsoft Office —and it probably is— choose the Windows Microsoft Office command from the Program Manager menu bar.

3 Double-click on the Microsoft Excel program item.

Starting Excel Automatically

To start Excel each time Windows starts, follow these steps:

1 Start Windows—for example, by typing *win* at the MS-DOS prompt.

2 Display the program group in which Excel is an item. For example, if Excel's program group is Microsoft Office —and it probably is— choose the Window Microsoft Office command from the Program Manager menu bar.

3 Display the Startup program group—for example, by choosing the Window Startup command from the Program Manager menu bar.

4 Drag the Microsoft Excel program item from the Microsoft Office program group window to the Startup program group window.

Statistics Functions

A statistics function calculates some statistical measure. A special variety of a statistics function—the database functions— even calculates statistical measures of selected values from an Excel list, or database.

Here is a sampling of Excel general statistics functions:

Function	What it does
=AVERAGE(2,3,4,5,1)	Returns the average of the values 2, 3, 4, 5, and 1, which is 3.
=MAX(23,456,12)	Returns the maximum value included as an argument, which is 456.
=STDEV(2,3,2.5,2,2.5,3)	Returns the sample standard deviation of the values included as arguments, which is 0.447214.

The general statistics functions accept a maximum of 30 **arguments.** Arguments don't have to be values or cell addresses, however. Arguments can also reference worksheet ranges. In this way, you can calculate statistical measurements for large samples and populations. (The worksheet range B1:B10000, for example, is a single argument that references 10,000 cells.)

 Function Wizard

Styles

A style is a combination of formatting choices.

Creating a new style—**Adding Styles**	
Deleting an existing style—**Removing Styles**	
Using an existing style—**Applying Styles**	

Subtotaling Lists
Use the Data Subtotals command to subtotal columns with values in a list.

Using the Data Subtotals Command

To use this command, you should first sort the list using the field you'll subtotal. Then select the list (including the header row) and choose the Data Subtotals command. Excel displays the Subtotal dialog box.

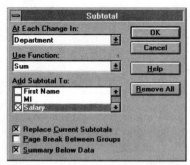

1 Use the At Each Change In drop-down list box to specify where subtotals should be calculated—such as subtotals by department.

2 Use the Use Function drop-down list box to choose which summary calculation Excel should make. (Usually, you sum, but Excel lets you make any statistical calculation: average, maximum, minimum, and so on.)

3 Use the Add Subtotal To drop-down list box to indicate which columns should have subtotals calculated.

4 Use the check boxes to control where Excel places new subtotal information.

5 Select OK. Excel subtotals the list.

Working with Subtotaled Lists

Using the default check box settings, Excel places subtotal and grand total information beneath the list.

	A	B	C	D	E	F
1	Department	Last Name	First Name	MI	Salary	
2	Acctg	Hapsburg	Jackson	A	$6,000	
3	Acctg	Ito	Fumio	S	$32,000	
4	Acctg	Johnson	Geoffrey	C	$20,000	
5	Acctg	Kirkland	Ralph	E	$47,000	
6	Acctg Total				$105,000	
7	Admin	Land	Walter	O	$22,000	
8	Admin	Mercedes	Marie	C	$47,000	
9	Admin Total				$69,000	
10	Mfg	Borchert	Shalandra	P	$18,000	
11	Mfg	Chang	Geng	Y	$36,000	
12	Mfg	DeLaurenti	Anthony	L	$34,000	
13	Mfg	Nagai	Patrick	T	$16,000	
14	Mfg	Olsenius	Aristotle	D	$47,000	
15	Mfg Total				$151,000	
16	Sales	Abbot	Peter	W	$14,000	

Employee Salaries / Department Payroll Summary

Use the 1, 2, and 3 buttons to tell Excel how much detail it should show in the subtotaled list. 1 tells Excel to show only the grand total. 2 tells Excel to show the grand total and any subtotals. 3 tells Excel to show the individual list entries.

To hide the individual list entries that go into a subtotal, select the minus button. Once Excel hides the list entries that go into a subtotal, it changes the minus button to a plus button. Select the plus button to unhide the list entries.

 Creating Lists; Sorting Lists

Subtotaling filtered lists

By subtotaling a filtered list, it's easy to perform many otherwise complicated calculations. Consider, if you will, the possibilities: You can count the times a particular entry occurs by filtering a list so that it includes only the entries you want to count. And you can tally a value field for a subset of list entries. All you need to do is filter the list so that it shows only the subset.

Switching Tasks To multitask, or run multiple applications in the Windows operating environment, you use the Control menu's Switch To command. Selecting this command displays the Task List dialog box, which lists the Program Manager, as well as any other applications you (or Windows) has started.

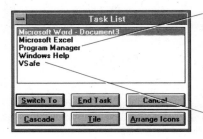

To start a new application, double-click the Program Manager. When Windows displays the Program Manager, use it to start another application.

To switch to an application already running, double-click it. Or select it with the direction keys or the mouse and then choose Switch To.

Using the Task List's buttons

Use the Cascade, Tile, and Arrange Icons command buttons to manage the application windows of the applications you've started. You can use the End Task command button as a last resort method for terminating a Windows application you can't stop any other way.

Tables ❖ What-if Tables

Text Boxes A text box is a box with text that floats over a worksheet or a chart sheet. Text boxes are, to be honest, the electronic equilavent of car bumper stickers. Even so, you can use them effectively to annotate worksheets and charts.

Adding Text Boxes

To add a text box, follow these steps:

1 Select the Text Box tool.

2 Drag the mouse between the initial positions of the upper left and lower right text box corners. Excel draws the text box.

3 Type the text that you want to appear in the box.

> **Save the Whales**

Resizing Text Boxes

Select the text box by clicking on its border; then drag the box's selection handles to change its size.

Moving Text Boxes

Select the text box by clicking on its border; then drag the box to a new location. (You need to click inside the text box before starting to drag.)

Removing Text Boxes

Select the text box by clicking; then press the Delete key.

Text Functions Most functions manipulate values, but Excel also provides functions that manipulate text. The textual arguments in a text function can be either addresses of cells containing text labels or text strings enclosed in quotation marks. Here are some example text functions:

continues

Text Functions *(continued)*

Function	What it does
=PROPER("mr. president")	Capitalizes initial letter of each word in string, returning Mr. President.
=REPT("Walla",2)	Repeats the first argument the number of times specified in the second argument, returning WallaWalla.
=LEN("Chrysanthemum")	Counts the number of characters in a text string, returning 13.

Argument; Function Wizard; Text String Formulas

Text String Formulas Excel formulas usually arithmetically manipulate values: adding, subtracting, multiplying, dividing, and exponentiating. (This last word doesn't appear in any dictionary, by the way. I just made it up.) You should know, though, that it's also possible to create formulas that manipulate text by combining text labels, extracting chunks of text from a label, and even changing the capitalization of the letters in a label.

To combine text labels—the simplest text string formula—you use the concatenation operator, &. With the concatenation operator, you can string together two or more pieces of text—including blanks. Here are some examples of text string concatenation formulas. Note that the third example assumes that cell A1 holds the label Dashiell and that cell A2 holds the label Hammett.

Formula	What it returns
="Walla"&"Walla"	WallaWalla
="Raymond"&" "&"Chandler"	Raymond Chandler
=A1&" "&A2	Dashiell Hammett

For other text string formulas, you'll need to use Excel's **text functions**.

Time Formats Excel provides time formats that you use to make time decimal values understandable.

Time Format Codes

Here's a partial list of some of the ways Excel lets you format an example time value, 0.75:

Format code	Formatted date value
h:mm AM/PM	6:00 PM
h:mm:ss AM/PM	6:00:00 PM
h:mm	18:00
h:mm:ss	18:00:00
mm:ss	00:00

Formatting Time Decimal Values

To format a time decimal value, follow these steps:

1 Select the cell or range with the time values.

2 Choose the Format Cells command and select the Number tab.

3 Select the Time entry from the Category list box.

4 Choose one of the time format entries from the Format Codes list box.

Note that near the bottom of the Format Cells dialog box, Excel shows how the active cell looks when formatted with the selected time format code.

Formatting Numbers; Time Values

Time Functions **Date and Time Functions**

Time Values Excel lets you use decimal values to represent times: 0 represents 12:00 AM, 0.25 represents 6:00 AM, 0.5 represents 12:00 PM, and so forth. Time values let you easily perform arithmetic using times. For example, you can calculate the number of hours someone works if that person starts at 6:00 AM and works until 3:30 PM.

Formulas; Time Formats

continues

Time Values *(continued)*

Date and time combinations

Combine date integer values with time decimal values to show both the date and the time. For example, to represent 12:00 PM on October 28, 1995, you use the value 35000.5. The integer portion of the value, 35000, is the date value for October 28, 1995. The decimal portion of the value, 0.5, is the time value for 12:00 PM.

TipWizard
You can tell Excel you want pointers while you work. Excel's TipWizard will then provide a list of tips, hints, and pointers related to whatever you're working on.

Displaying the TipWizard's Tip List

To display a list box packed with Excel tips, select the TipWizard tool.

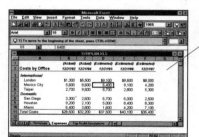

Click on the up and down arrows to scroll through the tip list.

Removing the TipWizard's Tip List

When you press the TipWizard tool, Excel depresses the button to show that the TipWizard is busily working away. To remove the TipWizard's tip list, select the TipWizard toolbar button again.

✦ Help

Toolbars
Toolbars are those rows of buttons and boxes that appear at the top of your window just below the menu bar. Excel initially places the Standard toolbar and the Formatting toolbar in its application window. But Excel also provides several other toolbars.

Adding and Removing Toolbars

You can add and remove any toolbars by pointing to the toolbar, clicking the right mouse button (instead of the usual left button), and then—when Excel displays a list of the available toolbars—selecting the one you want. (You can also use the View Toolbars command to accomplish the same thing.)

Toolbar button names

If you place the mouse just below a toolbar button, Excel displays the button name in a tiny yellow box.

TrueType TrueType is Microsoft Corporation's scalable font technology. If you're working with Excel, using TrueType fonts in your documents delivers a major benefit. Because of the way a scalable font is created, it's easy for Excel to change, or rescale, the point size in a way that results in legible fonts. Excel identifies TrueType fonts in the various Font list boxes with the **T** prefix.

⁞⁞ **Changing Fonts; Fonts**

Underline Characters You can <u>underline</u> characters in the current worksheet selection by pressing Ctrl+U or clicking the Formatting toolbar's Underline button. You can also use the Format Cell command and its Font tab options.

⁞⁞ **Changing Fonts**

Undo You can usually undo your last change to a workbook by choosing the Edit Undo command or by selecting the Undo toolbar button.

After you choose the Edit Undo command, Excel changes the command name to Redo. Choose Edit Redo to undo the effect of choosing Undo.

⁞⁞ **Repeat**

continues

Undo (continued)

Irreversible damage

The Edit Undo command undoes workbook changes made with the Edit, Insert, and Format menu commands and some changes made with the Data menu commands. The command also undoes workbook changes made by entering or editing data in cells. The Edit Undo command doesn't undo all workbook changes, however. For example, you can't undo workbook changes made with File menu commands.

Values
A value is a number you enter into a cell that you want to later use in a formula. In general, a value includes the numbers 1, 2, 3, 4, 5, 6, 7, 8, 9, and 0 and the period symbol to indicate a decimal point if needed. You can also include numeric formatting with a value—for example, currency symbols and commas—if you want Excel to use the formatting to display the value.

⁘ **Entering Data; Formatting Numbers; Labels**

Views
You can tell Excel to remember the way a worksheet appears in the workbook window: its size, position, displayed area, and so on.

Creating a View

You can create a view by choosing the View View Manager command and then selecting the Add button. Microsoft Excel displays the Add View dialog box, which you use to name the view.

Name the view using the Name text box.

Using a View

To see the view, choose the View View Manager command, select the view, and then select the Show button.

Visual Basic Visual Basic is Excel's built-in programming language. Visual Basic is way cool. It's also way, way beyond the scope of this book.

    ∴ **Macro**

What-if Tables What-if tables show a series of calculations using the same formula but a different value for each calculation. You might use a What-if table, for example, to forecast the different future value amounts you accumulate in a retirement account based on different annual contributions.

Creating a What-if Table

	A	B
1		$0.00
2	2000	
3	2500	
4	3750	

Leave an input cell at the left corner of the What-if table; Excel needs this for the calculations.

Enter the What-if formula next to the input cell. The formula should reference the empty cell and any other needed inputs. This formula, for example, uses the future value function =FV(0.1,35,-A1).

Enter the input values for the What-if calculations in the column beneath the input cell.

continues

129

What-if Tables (continued)

Performing What-if Analysis

Once you've set up the What-if table, follow these steps:

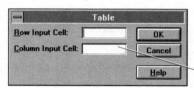

1 Select the What-if table.

2 Choose the Data Table command.

3 Use the Column Input Cell text box to identify the What-if input cell.

4 Select OK.

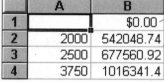

Excel uses the What-if formula to calculate results for each of the input values and then places these values in the cells beneath the What-if formula.

The future value amount accumulated based on $2,000 a year contribution, a 10% annual return, and 35 years of contributions is $542,048.74.

∴ Function Wizard

Table recalculation

Excel uses a special function, =TABLE(), to calculate the What-if formula values. If you change an input, Excel recalculates the What-if table value that uses the input. For example, if you want to see the future value amount accumulated based on a $5,000 a year contribution, change the value in cell A4 to 5000.

Window Command Buttons Arranged around the outside edge of the Excel **application window** and the workbook **document windows** are command buttons. You can use these command buttons to display the Control menu, to close windows, and to minimize and change window size.

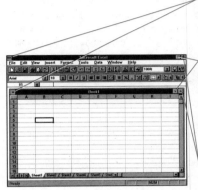

Click these buttons, called the Control menu boxes, to display a window's Control menu.

Click these buttons to minimize a window so it appears only as a icon. (Minimized document, or workbook, windows appear as icons at the bottom of the application window.)

The Maximize and Restore buttons' appearance depends on the window's size. If a window isn't maximized, click the button, which looks like an upward pointing arrow head, to maximize. If a window is maximized, click the button, which is a double-headed arrow head, to restore a window to its usual, unmaximized size.

A quick exit

You can close a document window by double-clicking its Control-menu box. You can also close an application window by double-clicking its Control menu box.

131

Window Control-menu Commands
To control windows and dialog boxes, you use Control-menu commands. These commands appear, not surprisingly, on the Control menus of **application windows, document windows,** and **dialog boxes.**

Activating a Window's Control Menu
To activate the Control menu of a window or dialog box, you click the Control-menu box. (It's the little hyphen-in-a-box in the upper left corner of the window or the dialog box.) Control-menu commands let you perform several operations on the window or the dialog box.

Restore	
Move	
Size	
Minimize	
Maximize	
Close	Alt+F4
Switch To...	Ctrl+Esc

Using the Restore Command
This command undoes the last minimize or maximize command, which is handy if you're fooling around with the Control menu, and you make a terrible mistake.

Using the Move Command
This command tells Windows you want to move the window or the dialog box. Windows, ever mindful of your feelings, changes the mouse pointer to a four-headed arrow. Once this happens, use the Up and Down direction keys to change the window or dialog box's position on your screen.

Using the Size Command
This command tells Windows you want to change the size of the window. When you choose this command, Windows changes the mouse pointer to a four-headed arrow. You change the window size by using the Up and Down direction keys to move the bottom border and the Left and Right direction keys to move the right border.

W

Using the Minimize Command

The Minimize command tells Windows in no uncertain terms that it should remove the window from the screen. Windows follows your command, but to remind you of the minimized window, it displays a tiny picture, called an icon. Because you can't see the Control-menu box of a minimized window, you simply click a minimized window icon to display its Control menu.

Using the Maximize Command

This command tells Windows that it should make the window or the dialog box as big as it can. If you maximize an application window—such as Excel's—Windows makes the application window as big as your screen. If you maximize a document window, it fills the application window. (In Excel, document windows hold workbooks.)

Using the Close Command

The Close command removes the window or the dialog box from the screen. There's more to this command than first meets the eye, however. If you close an application window, you actually close the application. If you close a document window, you also close the document, or workbook, displayed in the document window. If the workbook hasn't yet been saved, Excel will ask if you want to do this before it closes the document. Closing a dialog box is the same as selecting Cancel.

Using the Switch To Command

Cool. A power user tool. This command appears only on the Control menus of application windows. It tells Windows that you want to see the task list presumably so that you can start another Windows application—or activate another application you've previously started.

Application Window; Closing Workbooks; Switching Tasks

About the Control-menu commands

You won't always see each of these commands on a Control menu. Windows displays only those that make sense.

Window Panes

If you use rows to label columns or columns to label rows, you may want these rows and columns to stay visible—even when you scroll up and down and left and right in a worksheet. To fix the placement of labeling rows and columns, you turn the labeling rows and columns into panes. Then you freeze the panes.

Creating Window Panes

Position the cell selector at the cell below the row and right of the column you want to use as panes. Then choose the Window Split Panes command.

Freezing Window Panes

To freeze, or fix, the panes you create so that they label columns and rows even as you scroll down and right, choose the Window Freeze Panes command.

Removing Window Panes

To remove a window pane, choose the Window Unsplit Panes command. (This command replaces the Window Split Panes command once you've split a window into panes.)

Unfreezing Worksheet Panes

To unfreeze a window pane, choose the Window Unfreeze Panes command. (This command replaces the Window Unsplit Panes command once you've frozen a window's panes.)

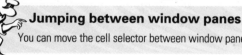

Jumping between window panes

You can move the cell selector between window panes by pressing F6.

Workbook Functions

Workbook functions return information about a workbook, your computer, or the operating environment. For example, the following function tells Excel to retrieve information about the operating system:

=INFO("osversion")

If you're using MS-DOS version 6.0, this function returns the string, "DOS Version 6.00."

∴ Argument; Function Wizard

Workbooks

Excel arranges **worksheets** and **chart sheets** into stacks of sheets—analogous to a pad of spreadsheet paper. Excel calls these stacked sheets workbooks; and it stores workbooks as files on disk.

New Workbooks; Opening Workbooks

Worksheet Pictures

You add pictures to worksheets with the Insert Picture command. When you choose this command, Excel displays the Picture dialog box, which you use to identify the picture file you'll add.

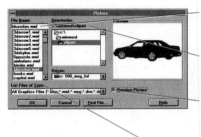

Use the File Name list box to identify the picture file.

Use the Drives and Directories list boxes to find the picture file.

Mark the Preview Picture check box if you want Excel to display a picture of the file in the Preview box.

Use the List Files of Type drop-down list box to specify which types of picture, or graphic, files you want to see listed.

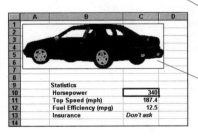

A worksheet with a picture.

Copying Objects and Pictures; Moving Objects and Pictures; Resizing Pictures

If you use Microsoft Word for Windows

If you use Word for Windows, you have a library of clip art images you can use in Excel. These clip art images are probably stored in the WINWORD CLIPART subdirectory.

Worksheets An Excel workbook consists of worksheets and **chart sheets.** A worksheet is the on-screen spreadsheet. Organized into rows and columns, it lets you easily build tables of labels, values, and formulas.

 Workbooks

Worksheet Titles Worksheet titles is a Lotus 1-2-3 term. It refers to rows you fix because they label columns and columns you fix because they label rows. (By "fix," I mean you don't want them scrolled when you scroll down and right in the worksheet.) Excel doesn't use worksheet titles. Excel does, however, provide Window panes, which let you accomplish the same thing.

 **Window Panes**

Worksheet Views You can control the appearance of the worksheet. To do so, choose the Tools Options command, select the View tab, and then make your changes.

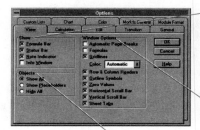

Use the Show check boxes to indicate whether you want the Formula Bar, Status Bar, Note Indicator, and Info Window to appear.

Use the Window Options check boxes to control whether worksheets show, for example, automatic page breaks, formulas (instead of the usual, formula results), and gridlines.

Use the Objects radio buttons to indicate how worksheet objects should appear. Show All displays the object. Show Placeholders tells Excel to display a gray rectangle in place of the object. Hide All hides the object and displays no placeholder.

Workspace A workspace is a list of workbooks. You can save a workspace, or workbook list, with the File Save Workspace command—in which case you save each of the open workbooks and the list of the open workbooks. To later reopen each of the workbooks listed in the workspace, you open the workspace.

continues

Workspace (continued)

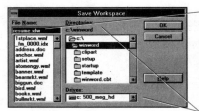

Use the File Name text box to name the workspace. You don't need to include a file extension; Excel adds the workspace file extension, XLW, for you.

Use the Drives and Directories list boxes to specify where the workspace should be saved.

Save Options; Saving Workbooks

Zooming You can magnify and reduce, or shrink, the size of the **worksheet** or the **chart sheet** shown on your screen.

Magnifying

Activate the Zoom drop-down box on the Standard toolbar. Then select a percentage. Selecting 200%, for example, magnifies everything so that it's twice its actual size.

Shrinking

Activate the Zoom drop-down list box on the Standard toolbar. Then select a percentage. Selecting 50%, for example, reduces everything so that it's half its actual size.

Actual size may vary

When you zoom a worksheet or a worksheet selection, you don't change the character point size, column widths, or row heights. You simply magnify or shrink the display. As a result, zooming doesn't change what your printed worksheets and charts look like. To do that, you use the Format Cells, Format Rows, and Format Columns commands.

TROUBLE-SHOOTING

Got a problem? Starting on the next page are solutions to the problems that plague new users of Microsoft Excel. You'll be on your way—and safely out of danger—in no time.

CELL ENTRIES

You Can't Show Long Labels

A label that is longer than a cell is wide won't fit in the cell. Microsoft Excel, however, is not without compassion.

As long as the cell immediately to the right is empty, Excel lets the long label, Kilimanjaro, spill over.

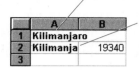

If this neighboring cell contains data, however, the displayed label, Kilimanjaro, is truncated to fit the width of the cell. Although the cell still holds the entire long label, only a portion of the label is displayed.

You can deal with cut-off labels in several ways.

Shorten the label.

You can shorten the label by editing it, for example. (Perhaps all you need to do is abbreviate some word.)

Use smaller characters.

1 Choose the Format Cells command.

2 Select the Font tab option for font and point size changes.

Increase the column width.

	A	B
1	Kilimanjaro	
2	Kilimanjaro	19340

And this is easy—simply choose the Format Columns AutoFit Selection command.

 Split the label into separate lines.

	A	B
1	Mount Kilimanjaro	
2	Mount Kilimanjaro	19340

1 Choose the Format Cells command.

2 Select the Alignment tab options and mark the Justify check box so that Excel splits the label into separate lines.

Aligning Labels and Values; Columns; Rows

You Can't Show a Value—Except as ######

If a cell isn't wide enough to display a value, Excel shows a series of # symbols. Take a peek, for example, at the worksheet fragment below.

In cell A1, the value 1000000 is too big to fit, so Excel displays a series of # symbols.

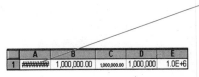

	A	B	C	D	E
1	#######	1,000,000.00	1,000,000.00	1,000,000	1.0E+6

In the other cells, though, I've made formatting changes, so the value fits.

 Increase the column width.

Choose the Format Columns AutoFit Selection command.

	A	B	C	D	E
1	#######	1,000,000.00	1,000,000.00	1,000,000	1.0E+6

continues

141

You Can't Show a Value... *(continued)*

Use smaller characters.

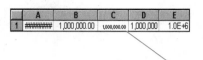

1 Choose the Format Cells command.

2 Select the Font tab option for font and point size changes.

3 Select a condensed font, if available.

4 Select a smaller point size, if appropriate.

Format the number with fewer punctuation characters: commas, currency symbols, decimal places, and so on.

This is just a matter of selecting a number format that uses fewer punctuation characters.

If you're using currency symbols and commas, for example, switching to a format that uses only commas will save a single character, the dollar sign.

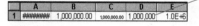

If you're working with two decimal places, but then switch to a format with zero decimal places, you'll save three characters: the two decimal places and the decimal point.

Use the General number format.

It converts values that are too wide to scientific notation. To use the General number format, follow these steps:

1 Select the worksheet range with the cells you want to reformat.

2 Choose the Format Cells command.

3 Mark the Number tab.

4 Select the Category All option from the Category list box.

5 Select the General option from the Format Codes list box.

 Columns; Formatting Numbers; Rows

You Can't Enter a Label

If you try to enter a label that looks like a value, Excel may enter what you type as a value—not as a label.

Add a label prefix.

You can force Excel to accept a cell entry as a label, however, by typing an apostrophe and then the label.

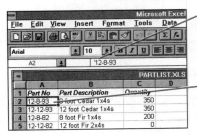

The apostrophe—which you can barely see here, so look carefully—tells Excel that this is a label and not a value.

This looks like a value, but really it's a label. If you enter it as a value, by the way, Excel assumes it's a date value.

continues

143

You Can't Enter a Label *(continued)*

Use the Text function.

If you don't want to include a label prefix, you can also use the Text function. Use the Function Wizard to build the Text function.

In using the Text function, you'll need to provide the value that you really want entered as a label and a number format, which should be used to format the value before it becomes a label. (If you don't know which number you want, simply specify the General format.)

You Can't Enter Anything into a Cell

If you want to enter something into a cell but Excel won't let you, don't worry. The problem isn't you. Someone told Excel to lock its cells. If the certain someone who did this has, like, half a clue, it probably means you're not supposed to be entering data into the cell.

Unlock the cell protection.

If you're sure you should be entering data into a locked cell, you can unlock, or unprotect, the cell. To do this, choose the Tools Protection Unprotect command. Excel may prompt you for a password if whoever locked the cells assigned a password. You'll need to give this password to Excel.

 Cell Protection

CALCULATING FORMULAS

You Can't Get a Workbook to Calculate

If you've set a workbook to manual recalculation (or someone in your office has—perhaps without your knowledge), you'll need to tell Excel when it should recalculate workbooks. Fortunately, Excel will tell you whenever it thinks you should consider recalculating.

Ready   Calculate

The Status Bar shows the word Calculate whenever a workbook needs to be recalculated.

Manually force recalculation.

To tell Excel it should recalculate the workbook, you can press F9.

Make worksheet calculation automatic.

To tell Excel it should automatically recalculate a workbook, choose the Tools Options command and then select the Calculation tab.

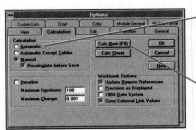

Mark the Calculation Automatic radio button to tell Excel it should recalculate formulas any time their inputs change.

You can also tell Excel to recalculate the workbook by choosing the Calc Now command button.

Calculating a single cell

You can tell Excel to calculate the formula in a single cell by double-clicking on the cell and then pressing Enter. Note, however, that if the cell's formula depends on the results of other formulas, these other formulas don't get recalculated. They may need to be recalculated, however, if their inputs have changed.

Excel Doesn't Recognize Your Entry as a Formula

If Excel looks at the formula you enter but doesn't think it's a formula, you've forgotten to start the formula with an arithmetic operator such as the equals sign, =.

Edit the formula.

Simply edit the formula so that it starts with an equals sign or a plus symbol.

 Formulas

You Can't Correctly Calculate a Formula

If you're just starting out, this can be mighty frustrating. But, rest assured, Excel is calculating the formula correctly. The problem, as painful as it may be to admit, is that the formula you've entered isn't actually the one you want to calculate. In a nutshell, your problem really boils down to one of operator precedence.

Override the standard operator precedence.

To force Excel to calculate in the order you want, enclose the calculation you want made first in parentheses. Then enclose the calculation you want made second in parentheses. Then enclose the calculation you want made third in parentheses, and so on.

 Formulas

A Financial Function Doesn't Work Correctly

Excel's financial functions are extremely powerful, but they're sometimes hard to use. Excel requires the function arguments to follow a very specific set of rules. If you can't get a financial function to calculate correctly, your situation most likely boils down to a problem with one of the arguments, as described in the following paragraphs:

Use a decimal interest rate.

The interest argument that most of the financial functions use is a decimal value. The interest rate 8%, for example, is actually the decimal value, 0.08. One of the more common mistakes new users of Excel make, unfortunately, is entering this decimal value as an integer such as 8. If you enter 8 instead of 0.08, you've actually specified the interest rate as 800% and not as 8%.

Use a periodic interest rate.

Forgetting to enter an interest rate as a decimal value isn't the only common problem people have with the interest rate argument. Another problem is not using a periodic rate. Almost always what this boils down to is using an annual interest rate in a monthly loan payment formula. But you can't do this. The payment periods—such as months—must agree with the interest rate periods. If you're calculating a monthly loan payment, you need to use a monthly interest rate. If you're calculating the principal balance on a loan with quarterly payments, you need to use a quarterly interest rate. If you're calculating the future value accumulated in a bi-monthly savings plan, you must use a bi-monthly interest rate.

Converting annual interest rates

In almost all cases, you can convert an annual interest rate to a periodic interest rate by dividing the number of periods in a year by the annual interest rate. For example, because there are 12 months in a year, if the annual interest rate is 6%, you can calculate the monthly interest rate by dividing 6% by 12, for a result of 0.5%.

Differentiate cash inflows and outflows with signs.

One other quirky but quite logical aspect of Excel's financial function set is that it requires you to differentiate cash inflows and outflows: Money you pay out needs to be included as a negative value, and money you receive needs to be included as a positive value. You indicate negative argument values with a minus sign.

continues

A Financial Function Doesn't Work Correctly *(continued)*

This sounds complicated, but really it's not. Take the case of a loan payment calculation made with the loan payment function. The dollar amount included as a loan balance amount is a positive amount (because you receive the loan from the lender), and the payment amount, calculated by the function in this case, is a negative value (because you will pay out the loan payment).

Here's another example. Say you will save $2,000 a year and want to estimate the future value you accumulate using the Future Value function. In this case, the $2,000 payment argument is a negative value (because you pay out this amount), and the future value amount returned by the function is a positive amount (because you will receive this amount at some point in the future).

Financial Functions; Formulas

PRINTING

You Can't Fit Something on a Printed Page (or Two)

Let's say you've got something that you want to fit on a single printed page—or even a couple of pages. Unfortunately, the print area is a bit too large. You've got two basic options for dealing with this problem.

Change the worksheet dimensions.

You can make a worksheet smaller by using shorter rows and narrower columns. Use the Format Rows command to shorten row heights. Use the Format Columns command to narrow columns. Note that you may have problems with labels getting cut off and values getting displayed as series of # symbols as you shorten and narrow.

148

Reduce the printed size.

If you don't want to change the physical size of a worksheet but only its printed size, you can tell Excel to fit a worksheet (or set of worksheets) on a specified number of pages.

1 Choose the File Page Setup command and select the Page tab.

2 Mark the Fit to radio button.

3 Use the Fit boxes to indicate how many pages Excel should print.

4 Select Print. Excel prints the worksheet on the specified number of pages, by reducing the worksheet size. With a little luck, you'll still be able to read what Excel prints.

Printing

Previewing pages

Remember, to see what your printed pages will look like, choose the File Print Preview command.

You Can't Tell Where Excel Breaks Pages

Microsoft Excel automatically breaks a big worksheet into page-sized chunks. If you're someone who's not all that fond of surprises, you may want to see where these page breaks will occur before the actual printing.

continues

You Can't Tell Where Excel Breaks Pages *(continued)*

Print Preview a workbook.

To get this information, choose the File Print Preview command and then close the Print Preview window.

Once Excel breaks a worksheet into page-sized chunks, vertical and horizontal page breaks display as dashed lines.

Print Preview

You Want to Cancel a Printing Workbook

If you've told Excel to print a workbook you later realize you don't want to print, you may want to cancel the printing. This is particularly true if the workbook requires many pages to print.

Switch to the Print Manager and delete the job.

When Excel prints a workbook, it creates a print spool file that it sends to the Windows Print Manager. The Print Manager then prints this print spool file as well as any other spool files that Excel and other applications have sent. To cancel a printing Excel workbook, therefore, you need to follow these steps:

1 From the Excel Control menu, choose the Switch To command—such as pressing Ctrl+Esc.

2 Double-click the Print Manager application on the task list.

3 Click the printing Excel workbook.

4 Click delete.

Printing; Switching Tasks; Windows Control-menu Commands

FILES

You Can't Find a Workbook

Sure, this is a bummer. But a lost workbook doesn't have to be as big a problem as you think.

Use the File Find File command.

You can usually use the File Find File command to locate lost workbooks. When you choose the command, Excel displays the Find File dialog box.

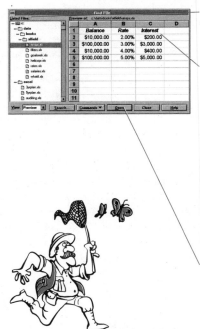

You can scroll through the list on the left half of the dialog box to find the workbook file you want.

Excel shows a picture of the selected workbook if the View drop-down list shows Preview.

You can use choose other Views too. The File Info view shows MS-DOS file information. The Summary view shows the information you enter into the File Summary dialog box.

When you find the workbook you want, select Open.

The first time you use the File Find File command

The first time—and only the first time—you (or someone else) uses the File Find File command, Excel displays a different dialog box from the one shown above. This dialog box lets you describe the criteria you want to use to search for workbook files. If you see this other dialog box on your screen and not the one shown earlier, describe the criteria you want to search for workbook files (probably *.XLS), the disk you want to search (probably your hard disk), and the directories you want to search.

You Accidentally Erased a Workbook

If you've just erased a workbook you now realize you desperately need, stop what you're doing. Don't save anything else to your hard disk. It may be possible to recover, or unerase, a workbook file.

Use the MS-DOS Undelete command.

How you unerase workbook files is beyond the scope of this little book: The mechanics relate to MS-DOS and not to Excel. So you'll need to look up the File Undelete command in the MS-DOS users documentation.

I will say this. When MS-DOS deletes a file, it doesn't actually erase the workbook disk file it just adds the workbook's disk space to its list of locations that can now be used to store new data. This means that eventually the workbook file data will be overwritten with some new file. But, if you haven't yet saved a new file over the old workbook's disk location, the workbook still exists. In this case, you can undelete the file.

 Opening Documents; Saving Documents

You Can't Remember Your Password

If you or someone else assigned a read reservation password to a workbook file using the Save Options command button, you'll need to supply that password from now on before you open the file. If you forget your password or can't seem to enter it correctly, Excel won't let you open the workbook.

Try a password with different-case letters.

Excel differentiates passwords on the basis of the letter-case. The following words, for example, are all different passwords from Excel's point of view: Wathers, wATHERS, and WATHERS. For this reason, if you think you know the password, try changing all the lowercase letters to uppercase letters and vice versa. It may be that you entered the password with a different combination of upper- and lowercase letters than you think. (This can occur, for instance, if you happened to press the Caps Lock key before entering the password.)

Opening Documents; Saving Documents; Save Options

WINDOWS AND APPLICATIONS

You've Started More Than One Copy of Excel

If you begin multitasking with the Control menu's Switch To command, it's not all that difficult to find that you've started multiple copies of Excel. This consumes system resources—such as memory. And it makes it difficult to share data across workbooks.

Exit from the active Excel application.

If one of the Excel application tasks is active—meaning the Excel application window shows on your screen—you can exit from it. (Do this with the File Exit command.) This closes the active Excel task, but the other inactive Excel task will still be open, or running.

continues

153

You've Started More Than One Copy of Excel *(continued)*

Close the second Excel task.

If another application or the Program Manager is active, follow these steps to close the second, extra Excel task:

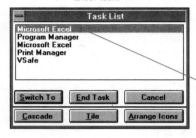

1 Choose the application Control menu's Switch To command—such as by pressing Ctrl+Esc.

2 Select one of the Excel applications from the task list— such as by double-clicking.

3 When the Excel application window appears, choose the File Exit command.

 Switching Tasks; Windows Control-menu Commands

You Can't Get Excel to Respond

It's unlikely but still possible that a bug in Excel or a bug in some other program will cause an application to stop responding. If this happens, you won't be able to choose menu commands. And you may not be able to move the mouse pointer.

Terminate the unresponsive application.

Unfortunately, if an application truly is unresponsive— if it ignores your keyboard and mouse actions—there's nothing you can do to make it start responding again. When this is the case, however, you can press Ctrl+Alt+Delete.

Ctrl+Alt+Delete—you press the 3 keys simultaneously —tells Windows to look at the active application and check for responsiveness. Windows makes this check and displays a message that tells you whether the application is, in fact, unresponsive.

```
This Windows application has stopped responding to the system.

* Press ESC to cancel and return to Windows.
* Press ENTER to close this application that is not responding.
  You will lose any unsaved information in this application.
* Press CTRL+ALT+DELETE to restart your computer. You will
  lose any unsaved information in all applications.

        Press ENTER for OK or ESC to cancel: OK
```

As the message text indicates, you can simply press Enter to close the unresponsive application. By the way, if the application isn't unresponsive, Windows knows this, and the message text indicates as much. In this case, you can press Enter to return to the application.

Patience is a virtue

Before you conclude that Excel or some other application is ignoring you, consider the possibility that it is just busy instead. Excel, for example, may be recalculating a complex workbook or running a macro or a Visual Basic module. Other applications may be printing to a spool file (which gets sent to the Print Manager for printing) or may be executing some command you've given.

You Get an Application Error

Sometimes an application asks Windows to do the impossible. When this happens—which isn't very often since the advent of Windows version 3.1, thankfully—Windows displays a message box that says there's been an application error.

Close the application.

When Windows does alert you to an application error, it usually gives you two choices. You can close the application, or you can ignore the error.

If you've been working with a workbook and have made changes you haven't yet saved, you can ignore the application error and then save the workbook. Save the workbook using a new file name, however. You don't want to replace the previous workbook file with a new corrupted workbook file. Then exit Excel.

If you haven't made any changes or haven't made changes you need to save, simply exit Excel.

QUICK REFERENCE

· ·

Any time you explore some exotic location, you're bound to see flora and fauna you can't identify. To make sure you can identify the commands and toolbar buttons you see in Microsoft Excel, the Quick Reference describes these items in systematic detail.

WORKSHEET MENU GUIDE

File Menu

New	Opens a new, blank workbook
Open...	Retrieves an existing workbook or workspace from disk
Close	Removes the active workbook's window from the screen
Save	Resaves the active workbook as long as you've already saved it once before
Save As...	Saves a workbook the first time
Save Workspace...	Saves all the open workbooks and also creates a list of open workbooks
Find File...	Looks for workbook files matching a specified description
Summary Info...	Displays information about the active workbook
Print Report...	Creates and prints specified sets of worksheets, views, and scenarios
Page Setup...	Describes the layout of printed workbook pages
Print Preview	Displays a window showing how printed workbook pages will look
Print...	Prints the active workbook
Exit	Closes, or stops, the Microsoft Excel application

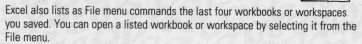

Numbered File menu commands

Excel also lists as File menu commands the last four workbooks or workspaces you saved. You can open a listed workbook or workspace by selecting it from the File menu.

Edit Menu

Undo   Reverses, or undoes, the last workbook change

Repeat   Duplicates the last workbook change

Cut   Moves the current workbook selection to the Clipboard

Copy   Moves a copy of the current workbook selection to the Clipboard

Paste   Moves the Clipboard contents to the active workbook

Paste Special...   Moves some portion of the Clipboard contents to the active workbook

Fill   Displays the Fill submenu

Down Copies contents of selected column's top cell into the rest of the column

Right Copies contents of the selected row's left cell into the rest of the row

Up Directs the gasoline station attendant to top off your car's tank

Left Copies contents of the selected row's right cells into the rest of the row

Across Worksheets... Copies contents of the selected group's first worksheet range into the rest of the group's worksheets

Series... Describes a pattern of values or labels that Excel should use to fill the selected range

Justify Arranges the active cell's text label so that it fits the selected range

Clear   Displays the Clear submenu

All Erases contents, formats, and notes of selected cells

Formats Erases formatting—numeric, alignment, fonts, and so on—of selected cells

continues

159

Edit Menu *(continued)*

<u>C</u>ontents	Erases contents—labels, values, or formulas—of selected cells
<u>N</u>otes	Erases notes attached to selected cells
<u>D</u>elete...	Removes selected cell, column, or row from worksheet
De<u>l</u>ete Sheet	Removes selected worksheet from workbook
<u>M</u>ove or Copy Sheet...	Changes current worksheet's position in workbook or duplicates current worksheet
<u>F</u>ind...	Looks for cell matching a specified description
R<u>e</u>place...	Looks for cell matching specified description and, optionally, replaces its contents
<u>G</u>o To...	Moves the cell selector to a specified location
Lin<u>k</u>s...	Describes, updates, and changes selected object's link
<u>O</u>bject	Changes selected object's border, background pattern, and protection

<u>V</u>iew Menu

<u>F</u>ormula Bar	Turns off and on the display of the formula bar. (Command is checked if the formula bar is displayed.)
<u>S</u>tatus Bar	Alternately turns off and on the display of the status bar. (Command is checked if the status bar is displayed.)
<u>T</u>oolbars...	Adds, removes, and customizes toolbars
<u>V</u>iew Manager...	Adds, shows, and removes workbook views
F<u>u</u>ll Screen	Alternately maximizes and restores the application and workbook windows. (Command is checked if the windows are maximized.)
<u>Z</u>oom...	Magnifies the workbook window by some specified percentage

Insert Menu

Ce**lls...**	Adds cells to a row or a column or adds an entire row or column
Rows	Adds a row to the active worksheet
Columns	Adds a column to the active worksheet
Worksheet	Adds a worksheet to the workbook
Chart	Displays the Chart submenu
	On This Sheet Starts the ChartWizard and adds an embedded chart to the active worksheet
	As New Sheet Starts the ChartWizard and adds a new chart sheet to the workbook
Macro	Displays the Macro submenu
	Module Adds a Visual Basic module to the workbook
	Dialog Adds a new dialog box to the workbook
	MS Excel **4.0 Macro** Adds a macro sheet to the workbook
Page **B**reak	Adds a page break left of the selected column or above the selected row
Function...	Starts the Function Wizard
Name	Displays the Name submenu
	Define Lets you add and delete cell and range names
	Paste Lists cell and range names so that you can use one in a formula
	Create Creates cell names using labels stored in adjacent cells
	Apply Tells Excel to replace formula cell addresses with cell names
No**t**e...	Attaches a note to the active cell

continues

Insert Menu *(continued)*

Picture... Adds a graphic image, or picture, to the active sheet

Object... Adds an embedded or a linked object to the active sheet

Format Menu

Cells/Object... Changes selected cell's/object's formatting, including its border, pattern, and protection

Row Displays the Row submenu

Height... Changes selected row's height

AutoFit Changes height of selected row so that cell contents are fully visible

Hide Hides selected row by making its height 0 points

Unhide Unhides hidden rows in selection by increasing row height from 0 to 12.75 points

Column Displays the Column submenu

Width... Changes width of selected column

AutoFit Selection Changes width of selected column so that all column entries are fully visible

Hide Hides the selected column by making its width 0 centimeters

Unhide Unhides hidden columns in selection by increasing column width from 0 to 8.43 centimeters

Standard Width... Changes selected column's width to 8.43 centimeters

Sheet Displays the Sheet submenu

Rename Names the active sheet

Hide Hides the active sheet

162

Unhide Unhides hidden sheets in the selected group

AutoFormat... Formats selected worksheet range by adding formatting for numbers, alignment, fonts, patterns, and borders

Style... Adds, changes, and deletes formatting combinations called styles

Placement Displays the Placement submenu

Bring to Front Repositions selected object so that it appears above, or in front of, all other objects on a sheet

Send to Back Repositions selected object so that it appears beneath, or in back of, all other objects on a sheet

Group/Ungroup Combines/uncombines all selected objects into a single object for purposes of formatting and repositioning

Tools Menu

Spelling... Checks the spelling of words in the cell labels of the active workbook

Auditing Displays the Auditing submenu

Trace Precedents Draws a thick blue arrow from cells with formulas to the cells supplying inputs

Trace Dependents Draws a thin blue arrow from cells with formulas to the cells supplying inputs

Trace Error Draws a thick red arrow from cells addressed by selected cell formula returning an error and a thin red arrow to cells with erroneous formulas that address the selected cell

continues

Tools Menu *(continued)*

Remove All Arrows Erases the blue and red arrows drawn by the Auditing commands

Show Auditing Toolbar Displays a toolbar of auditing tools

AutoSave... Turns on and off automatic workbook file saving. (Command is available if automatic file saving add-in is installed.)

Goal Seek... Calculates input cell value required for formula to return target output value

Scenarios... Adds and uses what-if scenarios

Protection Displays the Protection submenu

Protect Sheet.../Unprotect Sheet... Prevents/allows changes to active sheet and its contents

Protect Workbook.../Unprotect Workbook... Prevents/allows changes to workbook structure and workbook window

Add-Ins... Installs or uninstalls Excel add-ins

Macro... Runs a macro

Record Macro Displays the Record Macro submenu

Record New Macro... Adds a macro sheet so that you can record a macro

Use Relative References Records a macro's cell and range references as relative to the active cell

Mark Position for Recording Specifies where macro should be placed

Record at Mark Begins recording keystrokes and mouse clicks

Assign Macro	Tells Excel to run a macro when an object is selected
Options	Changes Excel's operation and appearance
Solver...	Solves an optimization model

Data Menu

Sort...	Arranges a list in alphabetic order using a label or in ascending or descending order using a value
Filter	Displays the Filter submenu
	AutoFilter Turns a list's headers into drop-down list boxes that you can use to selectively filter
	Show All Returns a filtered list to its previous, unfiltered condition
	Advanced Filter... Displays a dialog box you can use to specify filter criteria
Form...	Creates and displays a dialog box you can use to enter, edit, and delete entries in the selected list
Subtotals...	Summarizes entries in the selected list
Table...	Creates a What-if table
Text to Columns...	Starts the TextWizard, which you use to convert text files to workbooks
Consolidate...	Summarizes ranges of values in different worksheets
Group and Outline	Displays Group and Outline submenu
	Hide Detail Hides detail rows of selected worksheet range
	Show Detail Unhides previously hidden detail rows of selected worksheet range

continues

165

Data Menu *(continued)*

Group... Groups selected cells in outline

Ungroup... Ungroups selected cells in outline

Auto Outline Creates an outline

Clear Outline Removes an outline

Settings... Creates or updates outline settings

PivotTable... Starts the PivotTable Wizard so that you can create a PivotTable

PivotTable Field... Adjusts the properties of a PivotTable field

Refresh Data Updates a PivotTable's data with the most current worksheet data

Window Menu

New Window Opens a new window onto the active workbook

Arrange... Rearranges the document windows into tiles or a cascading stack

Hide Hides the active document window from view so that you can't see it

Unhide... Displays a list of previously hidden windows so that you can unhide one

Split/Remove Split Splits/unsplits the active document window

Freeze/Unfreeze Panes Splits/unsplits active window. If split, freezes the window panes above and left of the active cell.

The numbered Window menu commands

Excel also lists all the open document windows as numbered Window menu commands. You can activate a listed window by choosing it from the Window menu.

Help Menu

Contents	Displays a list of major help topic categories
Search for Help on...	Provides help on a topic you select
Index	Displays a list of help topics
Quick Preview...	Starts the online tutorial, Introducing Microsoft Excel
Examples and Demos...	Starts the online tutorial, Learning Microsoft Excel
Lotus 1-2-3...	Tells the Excel way to accomplish a Lotus 1-2-3 task
Multiplan...	Tells the Excel way to accomplish a Multiplan task
Technical Support...	Tells about support available for Microsoft Excel
About Microsoft Excel...	Displays the copyright notice, the software version number, and your computer's available memory

BUTTON GUIDE

Standard Toolbar

	Opens a new, blank workbook
	Displays the Open dialog box so that you can retrieve an existing workbook
	Saves the active workbook on disk
	Prints the active workbook

continues

Standard Toolbar *(continued)*

🔍	Shows what the printed pages of a workbook will look like
✓	Checks the spelling of words in the cell labels of the active workbook
✂	Moves the current workbook selection to the Clipboard
📄	Moves a copy of the current workbook selection to the Clipboard
📋	Moves the Clipboard contents to the active workbook
🖌	Copies formatting of the active cell to the rest of the selection
↶	Undoes the last workbook change
↷	Repeats the last workbook change
Σ	Sums worksheet selection, placing SUM functions in adjacent empty cells
f_*	Starts the Function Wizard
A↓Z	Uses the first field in a list to arrange selection in ascending value or A to Z alphabetic order
Z↓A	Uses the first field in a list to arrange selection in descending value or Z to A reverse alphabetic order
📊	Starts the ChartWizard

[icon]	Adds a text box to the active sheet
[icon]	Displays the drawing tool buttons
100% [icon]	Magnifies or reduces workbook contents by specified zoom percentage
[icon]	Starts the Tip Wizard
[icon]	Displays help information about whatever you next click: a command, a piece of a workbook, or some element of the application or document window. Very handy.

Formatting Toolbar

Arial [icon]	Changes font of workbook selection
10 [icon]	Changes character point size of workbook selection
B	Bolds characters in workbook selection
I	Italicizes characters in workbook selection
U	Underlines characters in workbook selection
[icon]	Left-aligns cell contents
[icon]	Centers cell contents
[icon]	Right-aligns cell contents
[icon]	Centers cell contents across selected columns
$	Applies the currency style to selection

continues

169

Formatting Toolbar *(continued)*

%	Applies the percent style to selection
,	Applies the comma style to selection
	Adds one decimal place to selection
	Removes one decimal place from selection
	Adds borders
	Colors background and fills pattern of selection
	Colors characters of selection

Charting Toolbar

	Displays additional toolbar buttons for changing chart type
	Plots 2-dimensional area chart
	Plots 2-dimensional bar chart
	Plots 2-dimensional column chart
	Plots 2-dimensional line chart
	Plots 2-dimensional pie chart
	Plots 2-dimensional XY, or scatter, chart
	Plots 2-dimensional doughnut chart

	Plots 3-dimensional area chart
	Plots 3-dimensional bar chart
	Plots 3-dimensional column chart
	Plots 3-dimensional line, or ribbon, chart
	Plots 3-dimensional pie chart
	Plots 3-dimensional surface chart
	Plots 2-dimensional radar chart
	Plots default chart type, a 2-dimensional column chart
	Starts the ChartWizard
	Adds and removes value axis gridlines
	Adds and removes legends

CHART MENU GUIDE

File Menu

New	Opens a new, blank workbook
Open...	Retrieves an existing workbook or workspace from disk
Close	Removes the active workbook's window from the screen
Save	Resaves the active workbook as long as you've already saved it once before

continues

File Menu *(continued)*

Save As...	Saves a workbook the first time
Save Workspace...	Saves all the open workbooks and also creates a list of open workbooks
Find File...	Looks for workbook files matching a specified description
Summary Info...	Displays information about the active workbook
Page Setup...	Describes the layout of printed chart
Print Preview	Displays a window showing how printed chart will look
Print...	Prints the chart
Exit	Closes, or stops, the Microsoft Excel application

Numbered File menu commands

Excel also lists as File menu commands the last four workbooks or workspaces you saved. You can open a listed workbook or workspace by selecting it from the File menu.

Edit Menu

Undo	Reverses, or undoes, the last chart change
Repeat	Duplicates the last chart change
Cut	Moves the current chart selection to the Clipboard
Copy	Moves a copy of the current chart selection to the Clipboard
Paste	Moves the Clipboard contents into the chart
Paste Special...	Moves some portion of the Clipboard contents to the chart

Cle<u>a</u>r	Displays the Clear submenu
	<u>A</u>ll Erases the selected chart part and its formatting
	<u>S</u>eries Erases the selected chart part
	<u>F</u>ormats Erases formatting—numeric, alignment, fonts, and so on—of selected chart part
De<u>l</u>ete Sheet	Removes selected chart sheet from workbook
<u>M</u>ove or Copy Sheet...	Changes current chart sheet's position in workbook or duplicates current chart sheet
Lin<u>k</u>s...	Describes, updates, and changes selected object's link

<u>V</u>iew Menu

<u>F</u>ormula Bar	Turns off and on the display of the formula bar. (Command is checked if the formula bar is displayed.)
<u>S</u>tatus Bar	Turns off and on the display of the status bar. (Command is checked if the status bar is displayed.)
<u>T</u>oolbars...	Adds, removes, and customizes toolbars
F<u>u</u>ll Screen	Maximizes and restores the application and workbook windows. (Command is checked if the windows are maximized.)
Sized With <u>W</u>indow	Alternately resizes chart so that it fills the entire window or fills half the window. (Command is checked if the chart fills the entire window.)
<u>Z</u>oom...	Magnifies the workbook window by some specified percentage

Insert Menu

Titles...	Adds titles to a chart and chart axes
Data Labels...	Adds text that describes plotted data points
Legend	Adds and removes legends
Axes...	Adds and removes horizontal and vertical axes
Gridlines...	Adds and removes horizontal and vertical gridlines
Picture...	Adds a picture to an active chart sheet
Trendline...	Plots a trend or regression line for selected data series
Error Bars...	Plots error bars for selected data series
New Data...	Adds a data series to a chart
Worksheet	Adds a worksheet in front of a chart sheet
Chart	Displays the Chart submenu
	On This Sheet Starts the ChartWizard and adds an embedded chart to the active worksheet
	As New Sheet Starts the ChartWizard and adds a new chart sheet to the workbook
Macro	Displays the Macro submenu
	Module Adds a Visual Basic module to the workbook
	Dialog Adds a new dialog box to the workbook
	MS Excel 4.0 Macro Adds a macro sheet to the workbook

Format Menu

Selected Object...   Changes the appearance of the selection. This command name changes to reflect the selection.

Sheet   Displays the Sheet submenu

Rename   Names the active sheet

Hide   Hides the active sheet

Unhide   Unhides hidden sheets in the selected group

Chart Type...   Selects one of the 14 chart types

AutoFormat...   Selects one of the preformatted versions available for the chart's type

3-D View...   Adjusts 3-dimensional chart's elevation, rotation, or height

Placement   Displays the Placement submenu

Bring to Front   Repositions selected object so that it appears above, or in front of, all other objects on a sheet

Send to Back   Repositions selected object so that it appears beneath, or in back of, all other objects on a sheet

Group/Ungroup   Combines all selected objects into a single object for purposes of formatting and repositioning

Formatting data markers

The Chart Format menu also includes numbered commands for each type of data marker used in the selected chart. You can format a data marker by selecting the marker's numbered command.

Tools Menu

Spelling...	Checks the spelling of words in a chart
AutoSave...	Turns on and off automatic workbook file saving. (Command is available if the automatic file saving add-in is installed.)
Protection	Displays the Protection submenu
	Protect Sheet.../Unprotect Sheet... Prevents/ allows changes to active sheet and its contents
	Protect Workbook.../Unprotect Workbook... Prevents/allows changes to workbook structure and workbook window
Add-Ins...	Installs or uninstalls Excel add-ins
Macro...	Runs a macro
Record Macro	Displays the Record Macro submenu
	Record New Macro... Adds a macro sheet so that you can record a macro
	Use Relative References Records a macro's cell and range references as relative to the active cell
	Mark Position for Recording Specifies where macro should be placed
	Record at Mark Begins recording keystrokes and mouse clicks
Assign Macro	Tells Excel to run a macro when an object is selected
Options	Changes Excel's operation and appearance

Window Menu

New Window   Opens a new window onto the active workbook

Arrange...   Rearranges the document windows into tiles or a cascading stack

Hide   Hides the active document window from view so that you can't see it

Unhide...   Displays a list of previously hidden windows so that you can unhide one

Numbered Window menu commands

Excel also lists all the open document windows as numbered Window menu commands. You can activate a listed window by choosing it from the Window menu.

Help Menu

Contents   Displays a list of major help topic categories

Search for Help on...   Provides help on a topic you select

Index   Displays a list of help topics

Quick Preview...   Starts the online tutorial, Introducing Microsoft Excel

Examples and Demos...   Starts the online tutorial, Learning Microsoft Excel

Lotus 1-2-3...   Tells the Excel way to accomplish a Lotus 1-2-3 task

Multiplan...   Tells the Excel way to accomplish a Multiplan task

Technical Support...   Tells about support available for Microsoft Excel

About Microsoft Excel...   Displays the copyright notice, the software version number, and your computer's available memory

177

D

E

N

O

T

The manuscript for this book was prepared and submitted to Microsoft Press in electronic form. Text files were prepared using Microsoft Word 2.0 for Windows. Pages were composed by Stephen L. Nelson, Inc. using PageMaker 5.0 for Windows, with text in Minion and display type in Copperplate. Composed pages were delivered to the printer as electronic prepress files.

COVER DESIGNER
Rebecca Geisler

ILLUSTRATOR
Eldon Doty

COVER COLOR SEPARATOR
Color Service, Inc.

INTERIOR TEXT DESIGNER
The Understanding Business

PAGE LAYOUT AND TYPOGRAPHY
Greg Schultz and Stefan Knorr

EDITOR
Pat Coleman

TECHNICAL EDITOR
Cory Garnaas

INDEXER
Julie Kawabata

Printed on recycled paper stock.

Get Quick Answers with the Microsoft® Field Guides

Field Guide to Microsoft® Word 6 for Windows™
Stephen L. Nelson
208 pages, softcover 4³⁄₄ x 8 $9.95 ($12.95 Canada)
ISBN 1-55615-577-8

Field Guide to MS-DOS®
Version 6.2
Siechert & Wood
208 pages, softcover 4³⁄₄ x 8 $9.95 ($12.95 Canada)
ISBN 1-55615-560-3

Field Guide to Microsoft® Windows™ 3.1
Stephen L. Nelson
208 pages, softcover 4³⁄₄ x 8 $9.95 ($12.95 Canada)
ISBN 1-55615-640-5

MicrosoftPress